Come Walk With Me

A MEMOIR

Beatrice Mosionier

HIGHWATER
PRESS

Published by HighWater Press, an imprint of Portage & Main Press Ltd.

Portage & Main Press gratefully acknowledges the financial support of the Province of Manitoba through the Department of Culture, Heritage, Tourism & Sport and the Manitoba Book Publishing Tax Credit and the Government of Canada through the Book Publishing Industry Development Program (BPDIP) for our publishing activities.

09 10 11 12 4 3 2 1

Printed and bound in Canada by Friesens
Cover and interior design by Relish Design Ltd.

Library and Archives Canada Cataloguing in Publication

Mosionier, Beatrice, 1949-
        Come walk with me : a memoir / Beatrice Mosionier.

ISBN 978-1-55379-219-2

        1. Mosionier, Beatrice, 1949-. 2. MÈtis women--Biography.
3. Authors, Canadian (English)--20th century--Biography.
I. Title.

PS8576.O783Z463 2009   C813'.54   C2009-905271-7

AUTHOR'S NOTE
I have grown up with the word "Native" and have used it throughout this memoir to identify myself and others, rather than using more current terms.

In an effort to protect the privacy of those I write about I have changed some names.

HIGHWATER PRESS
100-318 McDermot Avenue
Winnipeg, Manitoba, Canada R3A 0A2
www.pandmpress.com

TO MY FAMILIES,
WITH LOVE

INTRODUCTION

IT IS SEPTEMBER 1984. I'm on stage at Kildonan Park, in Winnipeg, for the Canadian Women's Music and Cultural Festival. *In Search of April Raintree* has been published for 18 months; the school edition is to be published in December. I will be reading from a manuscript I've been working on, *Spirit of the White Bison*, and introducing my panel of singers and musicians, none of whom I know. As I wait to go to the mike, I'm thinking, "What am *I* doing up here?"

Earlier I had wondered if I should try humour for the introductions. But I'm not blessed with that talent. Jokes that fall flat would detract from the performances. So I decide on safe, straightforward, if boring, introductions. The performers' energy and music will liven things up.

As I get my cue, I walk over to the mike and begin to speak. The audience rises in a standing ovation. At first I want to turn to see who else came on stage. When I realize the recognition is for me, I'm shocked, then I'm overwhelmed by their generosity, but apprehensive of what they might expect. They don't know the real me. The posters for the festival describe me as "Beatrice Culleton, powerful Métis writer." I don't think I'm powerful. I'm a mouse.

I relish that standing ovation because I know that it will be the only one I'll ever get. *In Search of April Raintree* will be the only novel I'll ever write. Had I known I would write a story that was already so meaningful to so many, maybe I would have lived my life differently.

One of the performers I introduce is Alanis Obomsawin, a singer from Montreal. After our session when she asks to interview me, I learn she is also a documentary film producer for the National Film Board. I want her to meet my mother and Alanis decides to interview her, as well.

The following week we three get together. First she interviews me and then I leave them so she can interview my mother privately. Because of my trepidation and my ignorance of technology, 18 years will pass before I hear that interview. By then I have come to realize that pieces of my life were missing and I needed to understand my mother's life. I had never asked Mom and Dad about their lives, for fear of making them relive painful memories; but Alanis's empathy and warmth made possible what I didn't dare try. So I have placed elements of this gift — my mother's story, as she told it to Alanis — at the beginning of each section of this memoir, as both a mirror to and context for my memories.

part one

Walking Alone

AUGUST 1949 TO
DECEMBER 1966

INTERVIEW PART ONE

I'M 72 YEARS OF AGE. I was born in 1912, on the 5th of July. In Camperville.

My mother, she was the Indian chief's daughter. Her name was Isabelle Napakitsit, Flatfoot, in English, eh. And my father, they said he was a Frenchman. Louis Pelletier was my father's name. But I don't know where he came from.

I didn't know my parents because when I was three months old, my mother died. And I was, uh . . . Mrs. Frances Ross took me after my mother died. She breastfed me and I stayed with them until I was two or three years old. Well, she was a Métis, but she married an Indian guy. And they brought me to that Indian school there, in Camperville. And the nuns took care of me, in that school. Sometimes it was, oh, that time... I'm alive now. But, oh, I took it, you know, because I was an orphan, and I didn't know any better.

Oh, I didn't even know my father. It was too far for him to come [visit]. He married another woman, after my mother died. So he had to stay home. One time, I, uh, I must have been about three years old. And it was just like a dream to me, when you're small, when you're two, three years old, it was just like a dream when I seen him.

I wasn't pure Indian. I wasn't supposed to stay there in the first place because I was a half-breed, eh. And they used to come and get me to work in the garden, to pull weeds. Oh, I don't know.

Sometimes, it was bad, and sometimes, just . . . just like that. I was only small, eh, when the nuns took care of me. And then from there they used to talk to me in English all the time.

There was lots of girls in there so we enjoyed ourselves. The girls, they learned me how to talk Saulteaux. When we were all by ourselves, eh, we speak in our language. But in front of the nuns, we had to speak in English. If we were caught speaking our language, sometimes we used to get the strap.

[Later] they sent me to Lebret, Saskatchewan. I liked it there better than the other one. Because if you do something bad, of course, you got punished for that. But if you don't do nothing bad, eh, you're okay. They won't punish you or nothing, for being good.

I stayed over there about three years, three, four years. When I was in Lebret, that's when my father died. I must have been 16 years old.

I was over 18 years and they send me back to Camperville. It's not like somebody that has been grown with their parents. When I come out of the convent, I didn't have nobody to fall back on, I had to go to work.

I had to stay with Mrs. Frances Ross. But they didn't treat me good. I had to, uh, I had to work hard. A lot of times when I was staying at Mrs. Frances Ross, I used to go out to the bush and cry in the bush, "Why did God take my mother away?" That's the way I used to cry.

But after, my sister took me. And then after that, my other sister Angele, she was in Camperville. That's the one who took me. And then after, my other sister come to get me from Winnipegosis. She was married to Jim Thompson. And I stayed with them a year, I guess. After that I started to work out. I always had a job to go to, all kinds of work. I always had a job waiting for me. If this job was finished, I had another one waiting for me. Well, you have to work. It doesn't matter wherever you are. You got to help, you know, help out. That's the way my life was all the time. I worked.

I went to Ste. Rose. And that's where I met my husband. He was living there. I must have been about 22. He must have been about 26. And then, well, we went around for about two years, eh, before we got married. At McCreary in the Roman Catholic Church. Well, he was a good Red River jigger and he was a good violin player. He used to win first prize contests. Oh yeah. That's how I fell in love with him.

That's the time it was, uh, very tough times. That's the time Depression was on. We had to work hard for the farmers. Five dollar a month, that's all we got, and the government paid us the five. There was only one time I went to work at, uh, on the other side of Neepawa, Eden. That's the only place I got ten dollar a month. And I was working for the Chinaman's there. Not on a farm, in a hotel, like. And I got my room and board right in there.

Well my husband was cutting wood for a farmer out there, at the foot of the mountains. But I didn't work, me. We had a little shack, there. The guy that he was working for gave us a piece of land, to put our garden in. So we always had plenty of garden stuff. It's only meat and flour, sugar, tea that we had to buy.

I had my Kathy about a year, I guess, after we got married. Then I had Vivian, two years after that. Then, twice I had miscarriage. Yeah. We went back to Ste. Rose. There was no place to get money, lot of times my husband didn't work. Well, sometimes he would get a job from the farmers. And then after, we moved to Dauphin, when the war came. My husband used to work in the air force, in the. . ., at the [air base].

We had a little house of our own. We bought that little house. So that way, we got along okay. And we put money in the bank and we got along good. Cause I was working, washing clothes for the airmen. Sometimes my husband would bring ten bundles of clothes, eh. And I had to wash clothes, like this, on a board. Yeah. We save enough money to buy that little house.

That was, about three, four years, till the war was over. And then there was no work at the airport, eh. So my husband couldn't work. There were no more jobs. Then we had to move right into town. I used to get, like day work. And that's when my husband come into Winnipeg to look for a job. He couldn't find none. So, he left us over there. Uh, lots of times, we had, sometimes we didn't have any, hardly anything to eat.

7

And then, we come to Winnipeg. Vivian was six years old when I had my son, Edward. And three years after that, I had Beatrice. That was my last one. They both were born in St. Boniface Hospital.

I only had one room, for the whole bunch of us. Yeah, a little table, two chairs. We only had one bed, like that. My [older] two girls, they had to sleep on the floor. That's all the room we had.

And then my husband found a job at Pine Falls. That paper-mill company. So we moved down there for a while. But my husband couldn't keep a job very good. Oh yeah, he used to drink a lot. And he would leave us for a week, two weeks at a time. And sometimes, two months, three months. Yeah. So I had to look after my kids all by myself. But they gave me relief. The city of Winnipeg looked after us. I always got a job for day work. And then that's how I fed my kids.

I . . . he was kind of a flirty guy, my husband. He got after other women and I didn't like that, 'cause sometimes, he didn't support the kids. I didn't care about myself, but the kids, eh. And then after that, we got into arguments. And I started to drink. And then, that's the time he'd leave. And then, uh, that's when they took my kids.

Well, that landlady, she, uh, and my husband, he was after her all the time, eh. And she didn't like me, she wanted to kick me out on account of him, so I went out looking for another place. Here when I came back, they'd took the kids.

I didn't know what to do. I can't have my kids, I didn't want him around. I went to my cousin and I stayed with her. And that's when I started to drink heavy.

And we had to go to court. And when they told me I couldn't have my kids I burst out crying — right in the courtroom. I said if I had a gun I would have shot the whole damn works of them. That's how I felt.

Oh, my heart was torn into pieces. That's why today, I pity any mother if their kids were to be taken away like I had had.

— *MARY CLARA PELLETIER MOSIONIER*

CHAPTER 1

M E, SONNY — THAT'S MY OLDER BROTHER — Vivian, Kathy, Mommy, and Daddy, we live on Jarvis Street across from the train tracks. In the summertime, me, Sonny, Vivian, and Kathy, and all their friends play on the trains when it gets dark. We play tag and run up and down the aisles of the trains. We make lots of noise, yelling and laughing, and our feet bang on the floors as we run. I am the baby of my family, so everyone looks after me. I am never scared, not even the times when the big man comes and chases us home. I think he is playing too.

One nighttime I have a dream. Me and Daddy are in a big parking lot. A whole bunch of black and white birds with long mouths are coming closer and closer. They can stand up and are not afraid of us. They are taller than me but not my daddy. Daddy is holding my hand and we are backing away from them. I look up at Daddy to see if we should be afraid, but he is just staring at them coming closer. Then we are at a wall and we can't back up any more. I wake up. I never forget the dream. It is the first time I'm scared for real. And I'm scared because Daddy seems scared too.

Daddy tells us a story about the boogeyman. The boogeyman comes out at night and he looks for little girls and boys. And if he can catch them, he takes them home and eats them up. That's a scary story, but Daddy's not scared, so I like it.

Sometimes me and Sonny wake up early. We have to play quietly so we don't wake anyone else up. One morning he spots two breads up on the counter and decides we'll clean them for Mommy. He pushes two kitchen chairs over to the sink. He gives one bread to me. As we wash them, they turn into white sticky stuff. We try to get it off our hands with the dishcloth and, after, we wipe that on our clothes. Pretty soon it's on our faces and in our hair and on the chairs. When everyone else gets up, they're not happy with us. I am the baby of the family so just Sonny gets heck.

Only me, Daddy, and Mommy are at home when a strange lady comes to visit. The lady is mad at Mommy. I don't know why. She is yelling and Mommy yells back. I am sitting on Daddy's lap at the kitchen table. He is watching them and laughing. I don't know why he doesn't make that lady go away. The lady is big and she pushes Mommy. Mommy pushes her back. Then that lady pushes so hard Mommy bangs into the washing machine and falls down. She stands up again and they are yelling and slapping. First I am scared. Then I get mad at that mean lady. I slide down from Daddy's lap and kick that lady as hard as I can. Pretty soon after that, she goes away. I don't know why Daddy didn't help Mommy, but it makes me sad.

MAYBE WE STILL LIVE on Jarvis Street. We are all in a dark room. All the places we live in are dark. I don't know why. The door on the wood stove is open 'cause I can see the fire. I sit on Kathy's lap. Across the table, Vivian turns the handle of a meat grinder. I watch the squished meat come out of the holes. I reach over to clean some meat out of one of the holes with my middle finger. I feel a sharp pain and I scream. Something inside the hole bites my finger and I pull it out fast. My finger looks like the squished meat and it is bleeding, bleeding, bleeding and I am screaming, screaming. Mommy and Daddy take me to a hospital. When I wake up a doctor tells me he took some skin from my arm and covered the tip of my finger. Now a big bandage covers my finger and another one is on my arm. I want him to show me what my finger looks like but he says I have to wait.

ONE DAY WE ARE AT HOME, and then Sonny and me are in a big building looking at Daddy on the other side of a big see-through fence. We are so excited to see him but we can't get outside to talk to him. After he leaves, me and Sonny have to stay there.

THE HANLEYS' IS MY FIRST foster home. I don't know where they took Sonny and I don't know where my big sisters are. Maybe they are at home with Mommy and Daddy. I want to go home.

The Hanleys are rich. They buy me all new clothes. The dresses feel crispy and smell new, and the underwear and socks are so white and soft. They have an upstairs and, in the bathroom, they have a toilet that flushes, not a pail in a closet like at home, and they have a big bathtub. Sometimes they fill it with water and bubbles, and Mrs. Hanley or an older girl gives me a bath with soap that smells so, so good. They have a little spaniel dog that pees on the carpet every morning even though it gets heck.

I am three years old but I have to sleep in a baby crib. Two older girls sleep in the room too. One's got light brown hair and the other one has dark hair. From the way Mr. and Mrs. Hanley talk, the one with the dark hair is a "bad" girl. I think the Hanleys have an older son. He takes me for car rides. I sit on the front seat and I am too little to see outside so I watch his foot push the pedals. Sometimes we wait for a train to come, and he tells me to wave to the man on the train. I kneel on the seat and wave and I am so happy when the man waves back to me. The big boy ends the rides by telling me that I'm too heavy and his foot is getting sore from pressing on the pedals, and he takes me back home.

AN OLD, OLD MAN lives there too. His bedroom is upstairs, next to our big bedroom.

MR. HANLEY TAKES ME down to the basement and sits me on a high chair. Then he cuts off my hair.

MY BEST FRIEND IS NANCY. She lives one, two, three houses from us. She is older and she takes me to bible school, down the block and across the street. I like bible school 'cause they let us cut and paste paper and they have colouring books. They show movies on the wall, about Jesus and God. Jesus and God have really nice voices.

ONE DAY, I'M IN the front yard. I look all around me. Everything is brand new. I don't feel too hot and I don't feel too cold. I feel just right. Someone mows a lawn and I like the sound. I breathe in all the way and smell the grass that's getting cut. Someone is painting a fence and I like the smell of that too. I lie down on the grass and look up at the grey, grey sky. I smell something else. It's the earth. I roll over and pick some up. I breathe in all the way again, and the earth smells so good. I put some on my tongue. I know I'm not supposed to eat it but I got to taste it. And I am so happy — happy to be alive!

I know about dying 'cause I already asked Mrs. Hanley about it. I asked 'cause of bible school and the prayer I have to say every night: "Now I lay me down to sleep. I pray the Lord, my soul to keep. If I should die before I wake, I pray the Lord my soul to take." Mrs. Hanley says that means if I die while I'm sleeping, I'll go to heaven. Only good people go to heaven.

THAT OLD MAN UPSTAIRS, at first he reads me books and sometimes he tickles me and makes me laugh. Then later he tells to me to visit him in his room. I look at things on his dresser and shelves. There's a funny smell in his room. I don't like it but I don't say nothing. He wants to show me something special. He tells to me to climb up on his bed where he is lying down. His bed is way high up and he has to help me climb up. He tells me to lie down beside him. Then he pushes back the cover and he shows to me the special thing. I know what it is and I know what it's for. It's to put in a woman. He takes my hand and puts it on his thing. I know this is bad. I am bad. So I never tell anybody about it.

I AM SICK AND I have to go to a hospital. I have to always obey grown-ups. Vivian told me so. A nurse puts a bedpan in my crib. Then she tells me to pee in the bed. I don't know what to do. If she wants me to pee in the bed, why did she bring me a bedpan? I have to obey her, so I pee in the bed. When she comes back, she seems kind of mad and she changes the sheets.

The next time she brings the bedpan, she tells to me to pee in the bed again. I don't want her to be mad at me but I have to obey. Again she is mad at me. When she brings the bedpan one more time, she just puts it in my bed and walks away. So I use the bedpan. I know how to use a toilet, but she never asked me that. Back at the Hanleys', I pee in my crib so the old man won't touch me when he comes in at night.

ONE DAY MRS. GIRWELL comes to pick me up in a car. She's a social worker. She is the lady who drove me to the Hanleys' place to live. I love car rides and we go for a long one. She tells me I am going to see my parents. Inside me I am so excited but I don't let her see that. I don't know if Mrs. Girwell likes me or not. She doesn't talk to me very much. If she doesn't like me, and she knows I am excited to see Mommy and Daddy, she might not let me see them. So I just be very quiet.

We come to a Children's Aid building and she leaves me in a small room. Later a woman opens the door and says, "Eddie's coming up the stairs."

Eddie? Who's Eddie? I think she should be telling someone else. But then, Sonny walks in. That's how I find out Sonny's real name is Eddie. Eddie has thick, curly hair like Mommy. Mine is straight. And short. Vivian and Kathy and Mommy and Daddy come too. They bring us donuts and candies. Kathy and Vivian are almost grown up.

Everybody talks and laughs. I mostly listen. I tell them only a good thing about the Hanleys: they have a piano that makes music so I danced a jig for them. I don't tell about the old man.

When this visit is finished, I think we will all go home together. I wait and wait. When Mrs. Girwell opens the door and tells to us it's time to leave, I'm so happy. We all put our coats on to go home, but Mommy bends down to hug me goodbye. I can feel her wet cheek on my face.

Another time I'm in the back seat of Mrs. Girwell's car and I have to go back to the Hanleys' place. I see Mommy and Daddy walking down the sidewalk, holding hands. They don't see me but I'm so excited. This is like having an extra visit. Maybe Mrs. Girwell sees them but she doesn't say nothing. I watch out the back window and they get smaller and smaller. Mrs. Girwell makes the car go on another road and I can't see them anymore. I'm happy they are together but I wish I could be with them too.

At another family visit I find out that Sonny lives with an old lady in a place called King's Park. Vivian lives with a family in St. Norbert. Mommy and Daddy give me a panda bear and he is black and white, and I call him Andy Pandy. I sit on the floor and play with him and I hear Mommy and Daddy talk to Vivian about Kathy. Kathy doesn't come to family visits anymore. Children's Aid says she is a bad girl and they make her live with other bad girls. The social worker said Kathy runs away to go back home to Mommy and Daddy. To me, she is good for doing that. When I get older, I think I'll do that too.

When Kathy was at the family visits, me and her are quiet. Vivian and Sonny, they talk a lot and make us laugh. Vivian is my favourite sister 'cause she teases me and makes me laugh so much. Mrs. Girwell told me I can't go live with Mommy and Daddy. Maybe they are bad. I don't want anyone to know I think that so I can't ask anybody about it.

I ask Mrs. Girwell and I keep asking Mrs. Hanley if I can go live with Vivian. If I live with her it will be a little bit like to be at home. I will be so happy. And one day, it happens!

CHAPTER 2

I AM FOUR AND A HALF YEARS OLD. It's wintertime. Mrs. Girwell puts me in her car, with some boxes of my clothes and toys. We don't go for a family visit. We go a long way, to a house in St. Norbert. This is where the Chevaliers live. This is where Vivian lives! But only a boy is there. He's big like me and his name is David. Then a little boy wakes up from a nap. His name is Guy.

In the afternoon Vivian finally comes in. We are so happy to see each other. I meet two other girls that live here. Nicole is a little bigger than me. Lily is big like Vivian. They were at school and they have to go to school every day. I want to go to school too, so I can be with Vivian but Guy, David, and me are all too little to go to school.

I'm too shy to talk, except to Vivian. But when Vivian is gone to school again, I have to talk to Mrs. Chevalier and I have to play with David and Guy.

All the girls sleep in two bedrooms upstairs. At the top in the hallway there's a piano. The Hanleys had a piano and I know how to play it. I just don't know how to make music like the grownups. I have a little bed in Nicole's room. Nicole has a closet on both sides of the bed, and a desk and a window. That's where the roof is pointed, and lots of sunshine comes in. One time when Nicole was at school I got on her chair and I saw the driveway and all the way to the church.

Vivian and Lily sleep in the other room. At night when everyone is sleeping, I wake up and I call to Vivian to come and get me. At first she does. Later she tells me to just come to her bed. But I'm scared of the pitch-black hallway. Behind the stairs is an open space and it's dark there even when the hall light is on. There could be a boogeyman back there. Boogeymans only like little children, and that's how come Vivian isn't scared. I really, really want to get to her so I breathe all the way in and run across the hall so fast that the boogeyman can't catch me. Then I get in Vivian's bed and she covers me with her blankets and I feel safe and I fall fast asleep.

After school time Vivian takes me for walks with her friends. She has lots of friends, and they are always joking around and laughing, and they throw snowballs at each other. I never talk but I always watch. I like it that Vivian is the leader of them.

IN DECEMBER MRS. CHEVALIER is baking almost every day. She bakes all kinds of fancy breads. I watch her braiding one in a circle. That will make it taste really good. Then she bakes cinnamon buns, and the smell is so good it makes lots of spit in my mouth. I hope she will give us some for our snack time but she puts them all away.

One day when no one has to go to school Mr. Chevalier takes us for a ride and we come back with a Christmas tree. He sets it up in the living room and wraps shiny cords and lights around the tree and then he hangs shiny balls, all different colours, on the branches. When he's all finished the lights come on. The living room is like magic. Over the next days wrapped presents appear under the tree. I don't know who puts them there. Someone tells me it's Santa Claus and I remember him. One time Mommy and Daddy took us to a parade. Santa was in it, and it was so much fun.

Late one night Vivian wakes me up and helps me get dressed and we all go to Midnight Mass. When we walk the block to the church the snow sparkles. After Mass we finally get to eat some of that fancy bread. Then we all go to the living room. Mr. Chevalier hands out presents and all of us get some. We get to play with our presents for a while and then we go back to bed. I love Christmas!

After a few days the big kids have to go to school again. On weekends they take us across the river to the really big toboggan hill. By the time we get home our mittens are all wet and our hands and ears sting as we warm up. I don't care because I had so much fun. I love winter!

VIVIAN TAKES ME FOR a family visit. After, she takes me to see Charlie Bell and his wife. They know Mommy and are best friends, Vivian tells me. They give us the best chocolate cake I ever tasted. I fall asleep on the bus ride home and Vivian wakes me when we're in St. Norbert. She makes me promise not to tell anyone we went to see Charlie Bell. From that, I guess we're never supposed to see anybody but our own family. Maybe if Children's Aid finds out they won't let us go for family visits again. I like having a secret that only me and Vivian know. I hope we can go see Charlie Bell again.

I GET SICK AND I have to go to the hospital. I am in a very dark room and up at the high ceiling I can see big pipes so I think I'm in a basement. I hear moaning and screams and a noise that sounds like one of Mr. Chevalier's saws. Maybe they're sawing somebody's leg off. I am so scared. I don't know what's going to happen to me.

Then I'm in a different room, big with lots of windows and lots of beds. The other children here don't like me. They call me "little papoose" and "little Indian," and that sounds bad to me and they make whooping sounds. They are making fun of me but I don't know why. The doctor hears them and tells them to be nice. I think he feels sorry for me and I don't like someone to feel sorry for me. Later a nurse brings me some soft ice cream in a little container and a flat wooden spoon. I am happy to have that but I wonder why she is being nice to me. Maybe just children are mean. She tells me I got my tonsils out. I don't know what that means.

The next time I get sick I have spots on my arms and I feel like throwing up and I am so hot. I show Vivian the spots. She says it's small pox. The other big kids tell me people usually die from small pox. I ask Vivian if I'm going to die. She says she doesn't know but she doesn't seem worried. Then I think she is teasing me. When Mrs. Chevalier gets home

Vivian shows her my spots. I have chicken pox, not small pox. I won't die but I have to stay in bed for a long time.

WHEN I'M NOT SICK I get into trouble. Guy, David, and me play hide-and-go-seek. One time David and I both want to hide in the shower in the bathroom and we start fighting, trying to push the other out. Mrs. Chevalier makes me sit in a corner by the kitchen. I think David has to sit in another corner but I don't know for sure, so I am mad.

In the spring David and I play in the garden and climb the crabapple trees. I guess we hurt one tree because Mr. Chevalier gets really mad at us. We both get spankings. First David gets it and he cries out loud. Then it's my turn, but I refuse to cry.

After, I go to brag to Vivian, "I got a spanking and I didn't even cry." Instead of giving me a compliment or even feeling sorry for me, she says, "Then you should go back and get another one." I know she has just told me that I shouldn't brag.

At church Mr. Chevalier and three others always sit in about the twelfth row, and the rest of us sit in about the sixth row. I get into a bit of a fight with Nicole: we try to take a prayer book from each other. All of a sudden I'm lifted out of my seat and dragged back to the twelfth row. Mr. Chevalier plops me down on the seat and sits beside me. All the people in St. Norbert are in that church and see this. My face burns hot and I wish nobody could see me.

THE BIG NEWS IS that St. Norbert is going to have a sewer system and running water. Mr. Fontaine, the man who brings us water, won't have to come anymore. I'm going to miss him because he pushes me on the swing in the garage while the cistern fills up. I am sorry that the big machines push down the trees and bushes. They put big pipes in holes in the ground and then cover them up. Then they make cement sidewalks. I miss the wooden sidewalks because they made a nice noise when we walked on them.

Mr. Chevalier puts a flush toilet and a sink in the main floor bathroom and now water can come in the shower that was already there. Later they put in a new furnace and the coal room becomes a potato

18

room. We still use the outhouse in summer and have to wash up in the basement. But now Mrs. Chevalier has running water for laundry. On the sides and at the front of the house, they have gardens filled with plants and trees. I miss the old trees and bushes that covered the rest of the block.

In September I go to school. I am in grade 1. Our school is a convent across the street and the Grey Nuns live there. Some of the girls in my class don't like me and they call me names, just like at the hospital. At recess no one wants to play with me. After a while I make friends with a few of the girls in my class. I think I am the only Indian in the whole school. I am the only one who has brown skin. Sometimes in class we sing, "One, little, two little, three little Indians..." but that doesn't say why it's bad to be an Indian. So I don't know why those girls don't like Indians. They must know something I don't know. Even when people don't call me names, sometimes I can tell they don't like me.

One of the girls, Cassandra, is a little strange. Some of the girls say she's retarded but I don't know what that means. She has a television and she asks me to come to her place. I go because I want to see her house. It is the biggest house in St. Norbert. We explore her house for a while. It has three floors and a big porch on three sides. Grass spreads all the way down to the bushes and trees along the river.

We play for a while until *Wild Bill Hickock* comes on, and then a show about Indians. I think it is called *Morningstar*. It's about an Indian family in the olden days. That show makes me happy that I am a little Indian. After that I go to her place every Saturday. But one day she closes her eyes and tries to kiss me like grownups kiss. The way she looks when she does that makes me think of the old man at the Hanleys' place. I never go to her place again.

Mr. Chevalier got a whole bunch of wood for the woodstove in the basement. They opened a window and threw it in the basement part under the living room. Me and David have to stack it nice and neat along one of the walls. He hands me the small logs and I stack them up. I tell him that at the Hanleys' place I had one of all the animals in the world and that my favourite animal was a white buffalo. When I moved here, I said, they all followed me, but they stopped at the highway because they knew there wasn't enough room for them. That was a much better story than just telling him the Hanleys had a dog that peed on the carpet.

Vivian decides to move away to the Tetraults, another family in St. Norbert. Since I had begged to move to be with her in the first place, I am confused and hurt that she wants to move away. The lady at the new house is going to give her real piano lessons. I want to go with her so much but I don't think they would want me. Vivian is pretty and she has lots of friends. That's probably why they want her. I never say anything to her because she is so excited to go. But inside me I am so sad that she is leaving me alone. Maybe she doesn't like me so much anymore.

CHAPTER 3

AFTER VIVIAN MOVES AWAY Lily takes her place. In summer when the neighbourhood kids play dodge ball, she makes sure I'm included. And she takes me with her when she visits her friends. I help her finish her chores, like doing the dishes, so we can play. Lily is not Indian at all and she has really beautiful eyes. She's around Vivian's age, maybe 15.

Mrs. Chevalier celebrates my third year with them with a cake and three candles. I am a very slow eater. Everyone else is finished so Mrs. Chevalier brings out the cake and lights the candles. I chew as fast as I can as the candles burn down. Everyone is watching me and waiting. One by one the candles go out so I don't get to blow them out after all. But I like her for making this cake for me.

That summer Lily and I go to Camp Morton, somewhere near Gimli, on Lake Winnipeg. Maybe Mrs. Chevalier noticed how sad I am since Vivian left, and that's why I am at camp. We have arts and crafts time and storytelling time. Sometimes I wander off by myself, and one day on the beach near the water, I watch a dragonfly fighting with a bee. They're still fighting when Lily is at the ledge above me. She's a little bit mad at me and says everyone was looking for me. "Didn't you hear us calling and calling? Come on, it's lunchtime." I was watching the fight so much I never heard anyone. I go to her quickly and she helps me up the ledge.

I don't want her to see what I'm looking at because she might step on the bugs and then they would both be dead.

Not long after we get back from camp, the Chevaliers take in two sisters, Melinda and Marla Mann. Melinda is a year older than me and Marla is a year younger. The first thing I notice about Marla is her long curly hair and I hope Mr. Chevalier doesn't cut it. I hate it when he cuts my hair and I always make sure he never catches me crying. He shaves up the back of my head, like a boy. At the sides he cuts my hair so short that I feel like I have giant ears. At the front I have very short bangs.

Marla and Melinda's mother died of cancer and their father can't take care of them. At night I lie in bed and wonder how they feel. They will never ever see their mother again and now they have to live in a foster home. They must be so lonesome but at least they still have each other. They share a double bed in Lily's room, where Vivian used to sleep.

I turn seven on August 27th, 1956. Last year, Mrs. Chevalier didn't know if my birthday was on the 27th or the 28th. She found out from the social worker. Mrs. Girwell isn't my social worker anymore. I like the presents and blowing out the candles. You have to try to blow them all out at once and then the wish you make will come true. I can never think of a wish while I blow the candles out. I'm going to be in grade 2 when school starts. Melinda's birthday is on September 27th, so we're going to get another birthday cake pretty soon.

I HAVE TWO DREAMS about fighting a bear cub. It's about my size. I fight with the cub as hard as I can until I see that it isn't fighting back. It is being very gentle. I wake up ashamed for trying to hurt it.

IN OCTOBER OUR PARISH priest, Father Forest, dies. He was kind to everyone and friendly. If he saw us outside of church, he would smile and say hello to us. Nicole and I go over to the church to say some prayers over the open casket. Well, she says the prayers and I take a good look at him. It looks like somebody put lipstick on him and his face is a greyish pink. I watch his chest to see if it goes up and down.

Besides homework, we have to learn lots of prayers in French. We have to recite our prayers by heart to Mrs. Chevalier and it's hard to pronounce the words. Mass is in Latin. It's boring. I have to sit still and not fuss so I won't get heck in front of everyone. I don't understand why all the people go to Mass all the time.

We have to have catechism lessons to prepare us for the sacraments of Confirmation, the Holy Eucharist, and Penance. That means we'll be able to receive communion but we'll have to confess our sins. Catechism classes begin at the convent and continue at the church. What I like is that in God's eyes we are all equal. God wants us to be kind to each other and be good people. Now that the other students know this, maybe they will all be kind to me and not call me names anymore.

One day a woman no one knows comes into church with her children. We all turn in our pews to look. From their clothes they look very poor. The woman asks if her children can take the catechism lessons. I see the looks on some of the nuns' faces and on the priest's face. They look at the lady and her children like they don't like them, and the priest is rude. He tells the woman they have to leave. The woman looks sad. I don't know why the priest and nuns behave like that and I don't like it. We already learned that we should love each other. We're supposed to be all equal. I decide that this is not my religion because I don't think the priest and nuns really believe what they're teaching us. I will have to learn it and live it, but it is not mine.

At our class the priest tells us that the bishop is coming for the ceremonies. From the way he says this, the bishop must be a special person. When the bishop comes we are to file in, genuflect to him, and kiss his ring, then go to the pews at the front, girls on the left side, boys on the right. Genuflect and kiss his ring? I'm not going to do that. We have to genuflect to Jesus. That's fine with me. But kneel to a man? No one is more important than anyone else. The catechism lessons say so.

Mrs. Chevalier has got each one of us a white dress with a crinoline. I love crinolines. They make dresses flare out, like Cinderella's dress at the ball. I wish our dresses were long, like Cinderella's, but we're going to a church, not a ball. On Confirmation day we all walk together over to the church. Everybody in St. Norbert is there and the boys are in little dark man-suits. We have to file in with everyone watching. I become very shy. There are way too many people. I genuflect to the man like everyone else, and I kiss his ring. I am too scared not to.

AT THE END OF THAT summer Lily moves away and another girl moves in. Her name is Mary Flatfoot and she has a dead leg from polio. She has to wear a brace and at first I think she is named Flatfoot because of her leg. She takes my single bed in Nicole's room and I get Lily's double bed in Melinda and Marla's room. The first time I sleep in this bed I stretch out my arms and legs because I have so much room. I can make a snow angel in my bed!

AT THE BACK OF THE Chevaliers' house there's a new house now, and the Dorge family lives there. The two boys are about the same ages as David and Guy, and they often come over to play. Every day we go to their place to watch *The Lone Ranger*. I like the smell in their place. I think it's a new-house smell. Then the Chevaliers get a television set and the best part of Saturday afternoon is watching *Zorro*. I love shows with animals, like horses and dogs, and I like their freedom of being outdoors. Mysteries and detective shows make me think about good and bad. I like it when the good guys catch the bad guys. I do not like comedy shows, especially the *Three Stooges* kind. They make people laugh at someone else getting hurt. I watch *The Mickey Mouse Club* because of Annette Funicello. She has dark hair and sometimes she seems to have darker skin than the others. She could probably pass for an Indian.

In the beginning I believed everything on TV was happening for real. One time a man stabbed a woman and then her hand quivered as she died. I asked Nicole why the person taking the pictures didn't help her out. Why did he just let it happen? She tells me the people on television are actors. I try to make my hand quiver the same as that woman and I can't do it. I can't believe that people can pretend to laugh or cry. But the more television I watch, the more I believe they can.

Sunday nights the family watches *The Ed Sullivan Show*, after we do the dishes, clean the kitchen, and say the Rosary in the living room. In the warm months we say the Rosary outside. I like that better because I can watch the birds and the squirrels and not be so bored. Mrs. Chevalier begins to read to us about the lives of the saints and that makes Rosary time much more interesting. Sometimes I think I would like to be a saint too.

THE BASEMENT IS MY favourite place to play. Mr. Chevalier has a workshop down there in one corner and our play area is in another corner. Mrs. Chevalier has the other half for laundry, ironing and to do canning in the fall. For Christmas one year I get a cardboard cutout-doll that comes with beautiful paper evening gowns and clothes for around the house and for the office. Downstairs I set up a little place like a miniature theatre and spend hours and hours making up stories for her, dressing her up, and having her go to work and out to dinner and dancing.

I HAVE ANOTHER DREAM about fighting the bear cub. When I'm in the basement cleaning up and thinking about my dreams, I wonder why I keep fighting the cub even though I know it means me no harm. And then it comes to me: I have three animals who are like guardian angels. One is the wolf, one is the cougar, and one is the bear. With this comes a feeling of being very special. One day I will do something special.

What happens soon after is not the something special I'm meant for. We all go to another town. The adults are in one room sitting at a huge dining room table, and us younger kids are in another room playing games. Someone comes to get me, and takes me into the room where the adults are, to meet the priest. He's a special guest for the grownups. He picks me up and sits me on his lap. The table is covered with a huge white tablecloth and plates of good food. I feel very special that the priest wanted to meet me. But then the priest puts his hand under the tablecloth and moves it to between my legs. He goes on talking with the other adults and no one knows what he is doing. I squirm off his lap and go back to the living room. I am angry. That man is worse than any bad guy on TV.

I sit in the corner. I don't feel like playing anymore. I don't want to talk to anyone. I want to go outside and walk by myself but everyone will notice if I put my coat and boots on. I don't want to be here. I wish nobody could see me.

Just because he's a priest the grownups respect him. And trust him. If I tell on him, if I tell what he just did, they would be mad at me. They would say I was lying and give me heck for making up a bad story. I know that nobody would believe me, so now I am mad at everybody. He makes me feel dirty and bad because I have to keep what he did a secret. On television the bad men always get caught. In real life the bad guy gets away. And I let him.

Many nights I lie in bed and think about that priest. I've never told what he did in confession. I never ever confessed what the old man at the Hanleys' did either. I tried but I just can't make myself talk about it. I wonder if the priest knows who we are when we make our confessions. And I figure something else out. I am living in mortal sin. I'm pretty sure that what happened, with the priest and the old man, are mortal sins. Every time you take Communion, if you haven't made a true confession to erase a mortal sin, you commit another mortal sin. Now I have so many mortal sins that I don't even know how many I have. I don't know how not to take Communion in front of the Chevaliers.

I've been trying not to think about all this and the more I try not to, the more I do. Why did that priest pick me? Somehow he must have known I did something bad before. But maybe if he didn't pick me he might have picked someone else, so that part is okay, I guess. Maybe this is why I have three animal guides: to help me be strong for what I have to keep to myself.

CHAPTER 4

I ALWAYS SEEM TO GET SICK in spring when everyone is outside having fun. Lying in bed one day I hear shovels digging into gravel. I get up and look out the window in Nicole's room. Mr. Chevalier and some helpers are mixing cement to make a concrete sidewalk. Curious, I get dressed and go outside for a closer look. I wish I could help because it looks like a lot of fun. When Mrs. Chevalier finds me outside she scolds me because it's still cool and I'm already sick. A few days later I cough a lot and get burning hot and just want to get out of my skin. Mrs. Chevalier tells me I have bronchitis. When my fever goes up to 104 degrees, they take me to Children's Hospital.

My bed is next to a chubby boy. On Easter Sunday the Chevaliers visit and bring Easter candies and chocolates. After they leave I see that the boy next to me didn't get anything so I share my candies with him. He gets extra sick and the nurses rush him out of the room. Then one asks me if I have given him anything to eat. When I tell her what I gave him, she seems kind of mad at me.

Back at home I tell Nicole and she says the boy probably had diabetes and he's not supposed to have sweets or he might die. Die? Maybe I killed him! Now I've gone and broken the fifth commandment! Another mortal sin! What would a priest do if he heard all my sins at once? I give up trying to figure out how to fix myself. In the following days I tell myself that if Nicole hasn't told her mom, then maybe what I did isn't all that bad.

ONE YEAR CHILDREN'S AID gives the Chevaliers tickets for us to go to the Shrine Circus. Everyone is excited, except me. One time *The Ed Sullivan Show* was about a circus and a man whipped lions and tigers to make them perform tricks. I didn't like that. Lions and tigers belong in the wild, not in cages, and they should never be whipped. I refuse to go to the circus.

Another time, Children's Aid gives the Chevaliers tickets for a ballet. To me it doesn't make sense to dance on your tiptoes. I'd rather play tackle football than be stuck in a theatre seat. So I stay home with Mrs. Chevalier. She rarely goes on those outings. I think that's the only time she can have quiet time to herself. She knows I also like being alone sometimes so they don't force me to go. By now we all call them Mom and Dad but I'm not sure if they like that.

SO FAR THE ONLY SPECIAL thing about me is that I can't do what's easy for everyone else. I never learn how to skip double-rope. I never can get a Hula Hoop to go round and round my waist. I can't get a yo-yo to work. I can't get a baton to twirl even though I study Melinda's hand as she twirls it. She does it too fast. The worst is not being able to ride a bicycle. One year I sort of learn except that I have to keep both hands on the grips and I always wobble. At least in school I do as good or better than the others, but I don't care about school. I want to be good at fun things. The one thing I love doing more than anyone else is reading. I'm about the only one who sits at the kitchen table, looking through the encyclopedia books.

Sometimes when we drive from downtown, before we get to St. Norbert, Mr. Chevalier stops at a place where they give pony rides. The first time I'm so excited that my nose starts to bleed. They take me off the pony and I never do get a ride. For a while after that every time I get to do something exciting, my nose bleeds. But soon it stops for good.

NEXT TO HOME AND school we spend the most time in church. Sunday mornings are for Mass and Sunday afternoons are for Benediction. I think the first Fridays of the month are confession, and then penance, which is usually ten Hail Marys. Masses are now said in French and the sermons are said in French or English. More and more English-speaking Catholics have moved to St. Norbert, so we relearn all our prayers from French to English.

One time Marla is practising the prayers at the kitchen table with me. She's doing well until she comes to the confession prayer. From French the prayer translates to: " . . . through my fault, through my fault, through my most grievous fault." When Marla recites, " . . . it's not my fault, it's not my fault, it's really not my fault," I burst out laughing. Then we wonder why the priest has never corrected her.

WHEN VIVIAN LIVES at the Tetraults' I can walk to where she lives, so I still get to see her. When I'm eight, she leaves St. Norbert for good. I don't miss her or feel sorry that she left because I think she went to California to become an actress. She's so lucky not to have to be a foster kid anymore. When I get old enough I'm going to leave St. Norbert too. And next time I see Vivian she'll be a famous actress.

THE NEXT YEAR MOM MISSES most of our family visits but I never ask Dad why. Maybe she moved away and that hurt him. Or maybe he's the one who left Mom and he feels guilty. He doesn't seem hurt or guilty, but either way, he's the one who should talk about her. I'm sad Mom doesn't come. I think she doesn't care about Eddie and me. Maybe she only came to the visits because of Vivian. I think Vivian was her favourite. That's okay because Vivian is my favourite too.

Dad and Eddie have good visits talking all about wrestling and wrestlers like Whipper Billy Watson and Gene Kiniski. We saw Gene Kiniski at a fair once but I don't like wrestling, so I don't tell Dad and Eddie about seeing him. I liked the Bonnie Sisters much more. They sang folk songs in harmony. I just stay quiet and watch and listen. Since I can't talk about my secrets, I can't think of anything else that would be interesting. It's like I'm just waiting. Waiting to see what happens and waiting to go back home. Maybe one day I'll be washing floors and the social worker will come and tell Mrs. Chevalier that she's picking me up because my parents are taking me back. Then I'll run upstairs and pack my things and in the car I'll have a big grin on my face.

MARY SLEEPS IN THE single bed that I had used when I first came here. One of us busted the top corner off the attic door, so now there is a black hole there. One night we're all watching TV, and suddenly we hear a blood-curdling scream from Mary. We all race upstairs to see what's wrong. At first all she can do is point at the black hole and whimper. Then she says, "A monkey's hand came through that hole and it was ... it was reaching for me!"

"Oh, you just had a bad dream," Mr. Chevalier says.

"No, I was awake!" Mary insists.

"It was just a bad dream, Mary. Say some prayers and go back to sleep." Mr. Chevalier tucks her in and goes back downstairs.

Marla and I stay behind. Shivers are still running up and down my spine. I tell Mary about the time I used to sleep in her bed. One night I thought the shiny knobs on the closet doors across the room looked like eyes, and they were coming closer and closer. Finally I'd gotten so scared I yelled. Mr. Chevalier showed me that the eyes were really just the moonlight shining on the doorknobs and he told me to say some prayers and go back to sleep. That worked. I promise Mary that in the morning we'll take a look in the attic.

The next day we end up tidying all the boxes and trunks in that attic as we look for the mysterious monkey. I understand Mary's fear because I have my own night terrors.

One night the sound of someone scraping fingernails on the hallway wall just outside my door paralyzes me with fear. Other nights it sounds as if someone is coming up the stairs really quietly, because the stairs squeak. One time a single piano key is pressed, so I just know someone is out in that hallway.

Those days after I hear noises I watch everyone, trying to figure out who is creeping around during the night. I know Melinda and Marla are asleep in their bed, and Mary can't walk without her brace. Nicole usually sleeps through everything. David and Guy would never do that. In those days the doors are never locked so it must be someone coming in from outside. I want to catch whoever it is but when it happens, I get too scared to move. I hate being so scared. I take one of the stray cats up to my bedroom. Her purring next to my head soothes me and puts me to sleep. I never do find out who's making those night noises.

We always have stray cats around, probably because I sneak food out to them. We wear aprons in the kitchen when we eat, do dishes, and clean up. The pockets are good for when I have meat I don't want to eat. Later I feed it to the cats. But sometimes I don't see them right away and I forget about the meat.

Monday mornings, at 4:30 a.m., Mrs. Chevalier begins the laundry. That's when the French version of my name being yelled wakes me up. "Béatrice Mosionier! Come down here right now!"

Right away I know what's wrong. Mrs. Chevalier will be holding my apron in one hand and meat in the other. "What's this?" she'll ask, which requires no answer. Dried up like that the meat looks disgusting. Silently, I just stare at her for the longest time until she seems to shrink, and, exasperated, she'll send me back to bed. I keep telling myself I have got to remember to get rid of the meat before I put my apron in the laundry but I kind of know I'm going to forget again. And I do.

AT TIMES I FEEL TRAPPED. I'm waiting, always waiting. I know now that if you're a permanent ward of the CAS you could get adopted and become part of a family. But I'm a temporary ward. That means some day Mom and Dad could take me home. The Chevalier family is not mine. If they don't want me they can send me away. I found out that my parents drink and that's why Eddie and I are still in foster homes instead of going back home. If that's true I don't like Mom and Dad so much anymore. I still love them but I'm hurt that they might not love us enough to try to get us back. I don't understand why they can't just stop drinking and take us back.

31

The other thing I found out is, that Marla, Melinda, Mary, and I, we're all Métis. That means we're half Indian and half white. In westerns they call people like us *half-breeds*. I've been called half-breed but never in a nice way. On TV, they never say Métis. Maybe it's just a polite way of saying half-breed.

Mrs. Chevalier has a desk in a corner of the kitchen. She organizes all her recipes and writes letters and Christmas cards there. She's very organized in everything she does. When I go out on my own I am going to have a desk. Above her desk is a cabinet. I've been eyeing that cabinet for a long time now. I have a bit of a habit of snooping. I try not to but one day when no one is around, I climb up on her desk, open the cabinet door, and I find bottles that say: *Alcohol.* That means the Chevaliers drink alcohol! If it's okay for them, why is it so bad that my parents drink it? I don't understand that so I get suspicious of the Chevaliers. For a few days I try to think of what else they hide from us but I'm too lazy to think it out.

I still wonder about one thing. Why do they take foster kids in? Us four girls have to do the dishes every day after every meal. On Saturdays we wash floors and clean the basement, and in summer it's us who weed the gardens. And there are lots of other chores that only we have to do. What do their kids do? Mrs. Chevalier works very hard. She cooks all the meals, does the baking, all the laundry and, now that Vivian and Lily are gone, she does most of the ironing. Her kids, Nicole, David, and Guy, seem to have a choice. They can help out or not. We don't have a choice. I guess we have to earn our keep because this house is their house. All the things in it are their things, and the Chevalier kids are sharing their parents with us. Sometimes Mr. and Mrs. Chevalier tell us that we are part of their family, but if we have to earn our keep, then we're not really, are we?

Mr. Chevalier never did cut Marla's hair. He cut Mary's hair, but it was already cut like mine when she came. Mary speaks up for herself and now all our haircuts have ended. My hair is so used to being short that it never grows as long as Marla's.

MRS. CHEVALIER LETS ME pick out a Sunday dress from the catalogue. I choose an orange dress with short puffy sleeves, a square neck, and a two-layered skirt that flares out. I love that dress, even though later, I think I must look like a pumpkin in it. The Queen of England is coming to Winnipeg and the Chevaliers will take us downtown to see her. Nicole tells us, "When you meet the Queen, you have to curtsy."

Curtsy? No, no, no, no. I won't curtsy to anyone. Then I wonder what they do to you if you don't curtsy to the Queen. Still, I won't do it, and this time I won't let myself get scared like I did with the bishop. For the next few weeks I wonder how come the Chevaliers are going to get to meet the Queen. On the day the Queen comes, we drive downtown and end up in rows of people standing behind a rope. She's in the back of an open car that passes by and she just waves to everyone. I dressed up for this? One good thing is I won't have to see if I'm brave enough not to curtsy to her.

Here's what I know so far about my courage. In an encyclopedia book I find a picture of a coliseum from the Roman times that fascinates me. In it a tiger is eating a man. In the background are dead bodies and pieces of bodies and more tigers. Other people watch safely from the stands. The dead people are Christians who have refused to give up their faith. If I had to choose, I'd pretend to give up my faith because I would not want a tiger tearing me apart. So I have no courage. I am a coward.

SOMETIMES MRS. CHEVALIER cleans the rectory for the priests, and she and other ladies in the parish do the big cleaning of the church. That one is a big, big job and we help her. I don't mind because we get to explore every part of the church. At the back is a huge loft where the choir sits. I've always wanted to go up there, sit right at the front and look down on the rest of the people during Mass, so I'm really happy to finally get up there and have a look around. I eye the tabernacle and remember how I used to wonder how Jesus could live in that small place. Whenever the priest opened the door, I tried to see Jesus but the priest would just bring out a shiny cup. Then I learned that communion just represented Jesus and that was disappointing. Exploring the altar area would be sacrilegious, so I stay away from it. Later I am told to clean the washrooms in the basement. That's how I find out that they have urinals in men's washrooms.

To get to the washrooms from inside the church I have to go through the sacristy. The sacristy is the big room where the priests and altar boys put their robes on. After a wedding Mass, the couple has to go into the sacristy with the priest and altar boys and they close the sacristy door. That was the only time that the door was closed. When I was younger, I was sure there was a bed in there on a raised platform with drapes on the side, and that the couple had to have sex in there to consummate their marriage. I used to think if I had to do that, I'd never get married. When I do the cleaning, I find only a big closet with all the different shiny robes that the priests wear, and the rest of the area is open with no platform and no bed.

In the basement an auditorium-like space is under the main part of the church, except that the ceiling is not as high as in an auditorium. Under the altar area is the stage. One Thanksgiving Mrs. Chevalier had a part in a skit, and when she came onstage as a pilgrim lady, someone in the audience whistled at her. It might have been Mr. Chevalier. Lily was also in that play, and even though she's not Native at all, she played one of the Indians who helped the pilgrims. The fun of snooping around has to come to an end since I have to get back upstairs and do some cleaning.

ON RUE STE. THERESE they build a new elementary school beside the cemetery. This school is big enough for all the girls from the convent and all the boys from the boys' school. In the new school, grade 5 starts out well because our teacher, Miss Lord, gives us a tip for remembering the order of the planets from the sun: M. VEM J. SUN and his dog, Pluto. I try it out on the Great Lakes. From east to west: OEHMS – nothing. From west to east: SMHEO – still nothing. When they named the lakes they should have thought about this kind of thing.

In history we learn about Native people. We find out Louis Riel was a madman who was hung for treason. We learn about the savagery of the Indians and later the Métis. That would be us. We learn about the courageous explorers and missionaries: them. Those brave white men only wanted to bring a better way of life to the Indians, and what happened? They got tortured and massacred. From western movies we'd already learned how vicious Indians could be. I never minded the others rooting for the white settlers but I kind of knew why the Indians fought so hard. Even so I had cringed at knowing I came from those mindless killers. Now here in my history book is proof that we 'half-breeds' are just as guilty as the Indians from the movies. While we're learning about this I squirm and keep my eyes glued to the text because I don't want to see other kids staring at me with accusing eyes. They probably find me repulsive.

That part of history is over soon but the lesson has a lasting effect on me. I come from murderous savages, and now we're drunks who give our children to white people to look after. I come from people who are losers, so I am a loser. All those little kids in school and in the hospital knew this. How come I didn't? Not only am I a loser, I'm also stupid.

CHAPTER 5

IN JANUARY MELINDA, MARLA, MARY, and I have a talk and I discover that they have the same perception I have: we are the ones who do most of the work. Except for Mrs. Chevalier, that is, but she doesn't count. We decide to run away. I hope I don't back down at the last minute like I usually do.

I study the map of North America on the hallway wall. Since Vivian had wanted to be an actress, she must be in Hollywood and that's in California. So that's where we'll go. If we don't find Vivian in Hollywood, then we'll live in the mountains where it will be warm year-round. I know which way the Red River flows, and reason that it must flow to the south. Since this is winter and the rivers are frozen, we could travel a long way straight southwest.

We choose to leave on a Saturday and I pack for our journey. I pack a box with lots of toilet paper and lots of luncheon meat. I make sure there's room enough for the box and Mary and a blanket on the toboggan. On the day we leave, Melinda backs out. I write a note saying, "We don't want to be treated like slaves anymore."

We leave the note with Melinda to give to Mrs. Chevalier, and Marla, Mary, a stray cat friend, and I set out. Marla and I take turns pulling the toboggan over the frozen Red River. I don't know it, and in the end it doesn't matter, but we're heading north to Winnipeg. By the time it's getting dark, Mary is too cold to go on. Finally I give in, and Marla and I climb the riverbank to where we see lights on in a house. The man goes down to the river to get Mary. They give us some tomato soup then he drives us back to the Chevaliers'. We sit silently, terrified of what we are to face. I wish I had never left a note. As long as I'm wishing, I wish we had never run away.

When we get home, we get a major scolding. They have even called the police and one comes by that night. He asks me the questions, because of the three of us, I'm the oldest. I refuse to say anything and just stare at him. Finally he says, "If it's okay with your parents, I'll give you a dog if you promise never to run away again."

I love animals so I make the promise.

After the officer leaves Mrs. Chevalier pulls out my note and scoffs at it. I am angry with her for that. She should talk it out with us, make us see our problem another way, if we are wrong. Instead she'll probably have me moved since I am seen as the leader of our rebellion. I don't care if that happens because I don't feel attached to anyone right now.

The next day the man from across the river comes to return the toboggan and the supplies. Mrs. Chevalier's mad at me all over again. She says, "Can you imagine how embarrassed I was when he said he brought back our toilet paper?" I had forgotten about our supplies and now the man knows I lied when I said we got lost. Not only that. Nicole tells me that our running away was on the radio! So the kids at school are going to know what we did. At least they won't know about the toilet paper.

The other thing I had forgotten was the cat. I had to go back on the river to try to find her. I don't ask permission to go look for her because if Mrs. Chevalier had said no, then I would have to obey — or disobey. Out on the river I called and called, but I never did find her.

Right from that day when I had refused to speak to the policeman, a weird thing happened. At school whenever I have to answer a question or read from our readers, I am tongue-tied for what seems a very long time. I open my mouth and no words come out. I try to force the words out, but nothing. This is so embarrassing because everyone must be looking at me. Since no one makes fun of me, maybe it is only seconds, not whole minutes.

Whenever this happens I think about staring up at the policeman in silence, refusing to answer his main question: why did you run away? Mrs. Chevalier had my note and knew the answer, so it was up to her to talk. I was not going to tell an outsider about our problems.

Soon the four of us foster kids make another decision. We have been calling our foster parents "Mom" and "Dad." Melinda suggests that from now on we call them Mr. and Mrs. Chevalier. Since I never knew if they liked us calling them Mom and Dad, I'm all for it, even though it's a little scary because it'll show that we're not finished with our rebellion. The other thing we talk about is that we are the foster kids, and their children are their real family, so it's us versus them. It's not that we're going to fight with them. We all get along quite well. It's more like we know our place now, and it is not as part of their family.

ON THE MORNINGS WHEN just us foster kids have to go to Mass, we sit at the back, and when Mass ends we're the first ones out. One cold winter morning, instead of going up front for communion, Mary thinks she'll be really smart and sneaks out. Even though there aren't many people there and no one who would tell on us, the rest of us piously stay to the end. When we walk out of the church we see Mary at the bottom of the steps, bent over the railing. For some strange reason she decided to lick the railing and got her tongue stuck. While we're laughing our heads off we try to warm up the metal enough for her to get loose, but she still leaves of bit of tongue behind. Punishment.

ONCE THE WEATHER WARMS up, the policeman brings us the dog. I figured a policeman would have a German shepherd, and I'm greatly disappointed to see it's just a Springer spaniel. Since the yard isn't fenced, the dog has to be tied up. And since it has to be tied up, it is always barking. It doesn't take much barking before the Chevaliers think the dog should go back home. I'm not sorry to see it go. Still, the policeman kept his word, so I have to keep my word and never run away again.

By now I'm pretty sure that Mrs. Chevalier has decided to keep me because, if not, I would have already been moved. An idea comes to mind. When I was little I asked to move here from the Hanleys' to be with Vivian, and it happened. So maybe if I asked to move somewhere else, they would move me again.

ONE HOT SUMMER AFTERNOON Mary, Marla, and I stumble upon some old wood planks and part of what must have been a raft, washed up behind the Grey Nuns convent. I think that if we can nail these planks back together, we can repair the raft and ride on the river. So I go home and get a hammer and nails. Hammering nails in the hot sun sure makes the sweat run. It takes most of the afternoon and a couple more trips home for more nails before we're done. I save one long piece of wood to manoeuvre the raft on the water. Because the planks are wet, that raft is very heavy. The three of us tug and push until we get it into the water — where it floats for about a minute. I'm about to step on it when one side tilts, and it sinks into the mud.

Later that night I lie in bed thinking. If the raft had floated we could have ended miles down the river. And how was Mary going to get back? What if it had tipped or sank later on? None of us can swim. With her brace Mary would have gone straight to the bottom. What was I thinking? New plan: if the raft had floated, I would get a rope and tie the raft to a tree and then we could have sat out on the water and pulled ourselves in whenever we wanted to. There, all fixed.

DAVID HAS GOTTEN INTERESTED in hypnosis. I don't believe it works, but one day a whole bunch of us are gathered in Nicole's bedroom, and he asks kids to do different things and they do it. Then he asks one of the Dorge boys to imitate me. He looks like a broken-down old mare, head hanging low, as if the sinful secrets I carry aren't hidden at all. Everyone laughs except me, of course. My face is burning with embarrassment. Since no malice is intended, I'm not mad. I'm just shocked at what I look like to others and I try really hard to improve my posture and my bearing.

ON SOME OF OUR SUNDAY excursions Mr. Chevalier takes us to the Assiniboine Zoo. My favourite animal is the wolf and it lives in a narrow, long cage. The first time I saw the wolf I made everyone mad at me by hanging around its cage after they had all moved on. I feel so sorry for this wolf because it is alone and paces back and forth, back and forth. Its fur is matted and dirty, it's so scrawny, and in its eyes there's only a blank stare, like it's given up on waiting for a worthwhile life. This wolf is not at all like my powerful, healthy wolf guide, but I love it anyways, because had it been in the wild, it could have been powerful and healthy.

CHARLIE SPOONER IS A foster kid who lives with another family in St. Norbert. He is in a few grades lower than me and is the school bully. Almost daily he would get into fights with the other boys and we all avoid him. It is also said that he steals things. One Saturday he's prowling at the edge of our garden. As I watch him I begin to feel sorry for him because I know he has no friends. I go out to talk to him. At first he's not friendly at all but I keep at it and he begins to talk with me. We go inside the garage and sit on the porch steps and we talk for quite a while. I am amazed at how nice he really is. If everyone else knew him like this, he wouldn't be so lonely.

That talk gives me the idea to talk with other kids at a place I go to deliver eggs. Mrs. Chevalier buys eggs in bulk from a farmer and a few families in the village buy eggs by the dozen from her. I deliver them. Whenever I go to this one house the kids call me names — *"Regarde la maudite sauvage,"* and, *"pauvre petite Indienne"* — all sarcastic, of course. They make fun of the way I dress and there's always whooping sounds. Sometimes one of them jumps around in a circle, imitating an Indian dancing and they all laugh. The young ones learn from the older ones and call me names even when the older ones aren't there. The oldest one is bigger than me. He calls me a squaw in English and he intimidates me the most. When he's not around I get the younger ones to talk to me, so that soon he's the only one who still makes fun of me, and it becomes safe territory. But soon after that I don't have to deliver eggs there anymore.

AT THE END OF AUGUST I celebrate my eleventh birthday. The last part of my tenth year was not good. Mrs. Chevalier has told me that I'm moody and she doesn't know why. I don't even know why. Some days I get so frustrated, so angry, I want to get out of my skin, just like when I used to get fevers. I've had about four fights with my foster sisters and the real kids. To win, I started biting. I wanted to rip things apart, not people actually, just whatever it was that made me so angry. After the last fight Mr. Chevalier gave me a good talking to and I decided not to bite anymore. Of course, no one wanted to fight with me, anyways, because I didn't fight fair.

I think what brings on the anger is when someone tries to boss me around. To handle my anger I go for walks in the woods. I have to concentrate where I'm walking so I don't trip or get scratched by branches, and that takes my mind off the anger. Just being in the woods makes the anger go away. Sometimes Marla comes with me and sometimes a stray dog will tag along. Besides, thanks mostly to my foster sisters, we still have plenty of laughs so I'm not always miserable. While I've thought of asking to be moved, I haven't done it, even though it's sometimes tempting. I don't want to be here but I can't go home because there is no home to go to anymore.

For years I kept myself in a state of patient waiting for my parents to take us back home. In the beginning I used to imagine that we would all just be together and that was enough. After I began to watch television, I would picture Dad as courageous as my television heroes and Mom as loving, caring and protective. Kathy and Vivian wouldn't live far from us and they would visit. We'd all do things together, like have a big meal and talk and laugh. Afterward I'd be happy to clean up because it would be for my real family.

But Mom still doesn't show up for our family visits. Kathy and Vivian are long gone. Vivian never did go to Hollywood and I feel foolish for thinking that she had. So it's still only Dad, Eddie and me that have visits. Knowing it's too late for our family to be reunited at home brings on rages, I think.

The rages begin with intense restlessness. A few times I've scratched long red marks into my arms, but not often because that hurts, and it still hurts long after the rage disappears. I've taken to pacing back and forth as my restlessness turns to a rage so overwhelming that I seethe with hatred.

Sometimes I try to figure out who or what it is that I hate. I'm angry with and disappointed in my parents, but they're really not the ones I feel a rage against. It's not my foster parents, either. I'm pretty sure they're doing the best they can. It's not even the social workers. Except for Mrs. Girwell, I have liked all my social workers. And I don't like Mrs. Girwell because she's the one who took me from my real home and delivered me to the Hanleys' and that old man. When the rage comes I want to run away. But I made that stupid promise to the policeman. Never make a promise you won't want to keep.

I keep thinking about that 'running-away' note. Writing that note had made all the blame for our running away fall on my shoulders. Mrs. Chevalier had said derisively that it was all my imagination, that they treat us very well, and we should be grateful to be in their home. It was not my imagination: we did do the work. Yes, they treated us well in the obvious ways, like providing food and clothing, but they were also unfair to us. So I was not grateful. To my mind, they *did* treat us like slaves. Without that note, how else could I have gotten across our need for fairness? Mrs. Chevalier was just too intimidating to talk to. We were scared of her, at least I was.

In November the restlessness becomes so intense I need to do something, so I finally ask Mrs. Chevalier if I can move away. She says yes, go pack your things and move.

Huh? Well that sure takes me by surprise. I thought she would have to contact my social worker and the process would begin from there. Elated by the idea that I got permission to be free, I go up to my room, look through my stash of Halloween goodies, and decide on what I'm going to take. First I wonder why I always want to wander off in winter. Then I wonder where to go. I'll go into the woods, north of St. Norbert. Where will I sleep? Under the snow — I read about that in some book, probably about dogs. How will I eat after I finish the last of my peanuts? Must be some rabbits out there. Could I really kill one? Nope. And I can't think of a single thing to eat out there. And how would I survive the cold? I can't figure that one out either. So I put all my things back and decide to stay. And I think that was a pretty clever way for Mrs. Chevalier to handle my wanderlust — for the time being.

That year rescue from my rages comes when I'm given the responsibility of baby-sitting. At first it's for a couple who go to bingo on Tuesday nights. Then I get another couple to baby-sit for. He is a professor and they live on Pembina Highway, close to the university. He picks me up and drives me home. Beside his house is a pasture with two horses. That's why I was really excited to baby-sit for them. Since the children are usually ready for bedtime, I never get a chance to visit the horses.

MR. CHEVALIER SOMETIMES gets such bad back pains that Mrs. Chevalier makes mustard packs and puts them on his back. Sometimes he even has to miss work. Mrs. Chevalier never gets sick. I think she wills herself not to. With a husband and seven children to look after, she doesn't have time. If she doesn't feel well she probably just hides it.

One day I see her in the washroom taking some aspirin. She either gets very dizzy or her legs give out, but I'm able to catch her before she falls. I help her back to her bed, and then I go find Nicole since she's planning on being a nurse. Later when we're having supper, and she's still in bed, Mr. Chevalier tells me Mom wants to thank me for having helped her. She doesn't have to thank me. Nobody would have just let her fall.

AT SCHOOL MATH IS one of my lousy subjects, especially algebra. Nicole's in grade 8, two grades higher, and always knows more than I do. She gives me a formula to figure out: B/G x 9 mo = b. I write it on one of my scribblers so I can figure it out later. Then I hand in that scribbler to my teacher so he can check our homework. The next day he makes me stay behind at recess. He points to the formula on my scribbler and asks if I know what it means. Puzzled, I say no. From his attitude, I suddenly figure it out: Boy over Girl times nine months equals baby. My face burns and I get itchy. He asks me where I got it from. I say I saw it somewhere and I just copied it. After eyeing me with suspicion, he lets me go off to recess. I haven't lied. Nicole wrote the formula on our little blackboard at home and I copied it.

English is one of my A subjects, as are English-French and Phys Ed, which to me doesn't really count. When our teacher tells us to write a composition, I do one about a lightning storm. It comes so easily that I don't have to spend much time on it. The next day after lunch the teacher has written my composition on the blackboard. I'm sure I'm in for a humiliation. Instead he tells the whole class why this composition is so brilliant. Really? I'm just a B-student with Cs to As on my report cards. I'm so shy I don't want the others to know I wrote it. It is this composition that will make me think later that, yes, I could write a book.

CHAPTER 6

Late one night after baby-sitting, I am compelled by the mild night air not to go home to our hot, stuffy bedroom. I walk along the riverbank behind the convent. The full moon is reflected on the river, and the night air is full of the natural scents I love, of bushes and trees, tall grasses and weeds, and especially of the damp earth at the water's edge. I feel wild and free! I end up at the pasture where Jody Dennison keeps her mare and the Clarks keep their Shetland pony. After visiting with the horses, I go home to bed, happily carrying that short taste of freedom with me.

The next weekend after baby-sitting I go to the pasture again and bring two ropes for reins, which I tie to the rings of the mare's halter. I lead her over to the fence rail and climb onto her back. As she moves around eating grass, I sit there, enjoying the feel of her underneath me. After that, I spend nighttimes with the horses every chance I get.

Then, stupid me, I go and tell Marla because she loves horses too. She tells a friend and her friend tells another friend, so the next time I go night riding there's a whole bunch of us.

By coincidence we pick the same weekend night that Mr. and Mrs. Chevalier go out of town to visit her parents, leaving the Beaumonts, our neighbours, in charge if we need them. We all meet at the pasture around midnight. The others soon get bored just sitting on the horse and pony, so someone suggests we take the pony for a walk so we can take turns riding it.

We're behind our school when a station wagon drives by very slowly. It's the Beaumonts'. Oh-oh, they must be looking for us. We wait until it's out of sight and then Marla, her friend, and I take the pony back to its pasture and head home. The kitchen and living room lights are blazing. From the garage we sneak in through the basement window and wait there in mortal fear. Eventually Melinda comes down and tells us we're in big, big trouble. We'd better come upstairs because they're talking about calling the police. The police! We might get arrested!

The questions begin immediately: Where were you? What were you doing? I tell them where Marla and I were but don't mention the others.

When Marla had left to meet me at the pasture, she had stuffed pillows in her bed, but she left her kimono outside. When Nicole came home from baby-sitting, she found the kimono and then the pillows. Then she went across the street to get Mr. Beaumont. They must have thought we had run away again. They didn't know I would keep my promise to the policeman. Later we find out that Mrs. Chevalier was really upset at having to leave her mother early. Not that it would have changed anything because we didn't even know her mother was gravely ill.

Mrs. Chevalier sends Marla and me to the Dennisons' and the Clarks' to apologize for riding their horses. I could have lied and said it was so hot in our bedroom we went out walking. That would have been simpler. What would have been even simpler would have been if I never went night riding in the first place. Now I feel like a criminal. I think we could have been arrested for trespassing. Although we got lucky and the police weren't called, all the trouble was once again on account of Marla and me.

AROUND THIS TIME, Melinda starts buying make-up and nail polish. The popular girls in my class already wear make-up and do their hair up in beehives. Nail polish makes Melinda and Marla's hands look really nice, especially Marla's, because she has long nails. I try it too, but my stubby middle finger — the one I stuck in the meat grinder — ruins the look. I was never self-conscious about my middle finger before, but now I realize how ugly it is. From then on I try to keep it hidden so no one will notice it.

FOR THE LAST TWO summers we have been going to camp at Albert Beach on the east side of Lake Winnipeg. I love camp. The boys' cabins are on one side, and the girls' cabins on the other. In between is a very large cedar-smelling cafeteria where we all eat. Most times after supper we sit around a campfire, perform skits, sing songs, and tell or listen to stories. On rainy nights we play bingo in the cafeteria. Every day we go to Mass, have breakfast, wash up, and clean our cabins. Then we have swimming lessons. I'm the only one in my group who can't tread water or swim. Embarrassed, I say I can only swim underwater. One girl's quite impressed.

After lunch we have games and then more time in the lake, usually for water sports. After that the canteen opens, and we can buy soft drinks and potato chips or chocolate bars. I love that word, *canteen*. It makes anything you get from there taste better.

One afternoon we go on a long hike through the woods to another part of the beach where it's rocky, and we have supper there. For me that's the highlight of camp. A lot of kids get poison ivy and mosquito bites but I don't. That's one good thing about being part Indian.

At the beginning the priest chose a small group of us to be in the choir and I'm pleased to have been picked. In the choir is a boy who stands out from all the rest and I get a crush on him. A few days later I'm in the water and look over at the shore. And holy cow, there's Melinda sitting on the sand next to that boy, talking and laughing. Jealousy is a bad, bad thing back then. (It's still not a good thing, but when religion is on your mind, it's very bad.)

We're back at home and neither Melinda nor I will ever see that boy again, but I'm still feeling jealous. I provoke her into a fight, and we're punching at each other, when she suddenly stops fighting. I look at her face to see why and she's looking toward the kitchen door. Mrs. Chevalier is there, watching us. For some reason she doesn't scold me, and I decide again that this will be my last fight. I'm not jealous of Melinda anymore, either. Melinda never even knew that I had a crush on this boy since I never told anyone.

I ONLY HAVE TWO OTHER crushes in school and both boys are in one grade higher than me. One is a major crush and the other is a minor crush, and they are best friends. I sense Major likes me as well because he always seems to be staring at me, but we have never talked to each other. I don't know why he might like me. I'm not pretty, I'm as skinny as a rake, and sooner or later, he might see my middle finger. On top of that I'm sort of a tomboy.

Kitty-corner from our house is a large fenced field with a pony. I try to ride the pony but it always bucks me off. This one afternoon as I'm getting up for another try, I spot Major and Minor in the back seat of Mr. MacDonald's car — he's their Boy Scout leader, I think — and they're both watching me out the back window. I just pet the pony and head home, embarrassed.

That summer they have amusement park rides at the community centre. Major and Minor follow Melinda and me onto the Ferris wheel. Once it starts moving, they both begin to yell to be let off. My crushes on them waver because I'm so disappointed to see that they're cowards.

ONE NIGHT I'M BABY-SITTING for the MacDonalds. Mr. Chevalier and his sons and daughter are gone somewhere for the weekend. Mrs. Chevalier is baby-sitting somewhere overnight and Melinda is at a sleepover. Marla and Mary return home from a friend's place to what is supposed to be an empty house.

They come over to where I'm baby-sitting, scared out of their wits. They tell me someone is in our house. The MacDonald kids are in bed so I can't go check our house. Instead I phone home. Someone picks up but doesn't say anything. Trying not to sound terrified, I say I'm calling the police so he better leave.

Marla and Mary wait for me outside. At around midnight the MacDonalds phone to say they're on their way, so I phone home again to see if whoever it is will answer the phone again. I'm so shocked to hear Mrs. Chevalier's voice that I miss that one second I could have told her that Mary and Marla are with me and someone was in the house. Instead I tell her I was just checking to see if everything is okay.

After the MacDonalds get back, Mary, Marla, and I head home. The problem now is to quietly get Mary, who can't walk without her brace, and Marla up to the second-floor bedroom past Mrs. Chevalier's open bedroom door on the first floor. I piggyback Mary upstairs. We're really quiet until I bump into the chair in the hallway near her door. Because we're so tense, we giggle.

The next morning at breakfast, Mrs. Chevalier asks me why I had really phoned and before I can answer, she says, "I think you phoned because you were up to no good." It figures — the one time I'm not to blame I do get blamed. Later in the basement, we find rags that smell like beer but nothing to prove someone was in the house, so we can't explain to Mrs. Chevalier what happened. She wouldn't have believed us, and Marla and Mary would have also been in trouble. My other fear is that she might not let me go baby-sitting anymore, and I prefer to earn money at that than to get an allowance.

MR. CHEVALIER HAS BUILT a greenhouse out of old windowpanes that he has collected from job sites. Our house is surrounded on three sides by his collection of flowers and bushes and trees. He also presses leaves and flowers in old catalogues. Sometimes he shows them to me and tells me their stories.

On nice weekends he takes us out to the woods and he digs up plants and brings them home to add to his gardens. One time some cows passed by us. A beautiful black horse was herding them home. No people, just the cows and the horse. I wondered how the horse knew how to do that.

The gardens around the house are not for vegetables. The Chevaliers have two large plots for vegetables on the other side of the church and the rectory. We have to weed the vegetable gardens all the time, from spring to fall. In the fall we gather the beans, peas, beets, cucumbers, and all the rest. Baskets and baskets of them end up in the garage where we have to prepare them for canning. We have to wash all the jars in water with bleach, rinse them, and leave them to air dry. Then Mrs. Chevalier washes all the vegetables and does the canning, and we finally get to play. Her canning lasts us the whole year.

SPIDERS GIVE ME THE creeps. One of the reasons is that sometimes I find dead spiders inside empty stored jars that have their lids on. They must have squeezed themselves small enough to get in there, which means that we're not safe from them anywhere.

One time we're in the kitchen and Mrs. Chevalier sees a big black spider crawling up my leg. She whacks my leg with the dishcloth before I can panic. Then she steps on the spider and the sound of it being crushed makes me just as queasy.

Except for flies and mosquitoes, when I find bugs inside, I take them outside. Another time, we're in the kitchen and I'm the one with a dishcloth. We've spotted a fly on the ceiling so she gets the flyswatter. Suddenly I feel sorry for the unsuspecting fly. So at the last minute, I shoo it away with the dishcloth. I expect she will be angry with me, but she just looks at me. She seems to understand that, out of all us, I am the bleeding heart.

UNFORTUNATELY, MY HEART doesn't bleed for my parents. I've come to a cold-hearted decision about them. At the last family visit when Mom didn't show up again and I sat and listened to Dad and Eddie talk and laugh, I got to thinking that they wouldn't miss me if I weren't there. After visits Eddie used to take the bus with me. Sometimes Dad would get us pie and something to drink at the Chinese restaurant near our bus stop and then wait with us until our bus came. I had loved that. But he doesn't do that anymore and Eddie doesn't take the bus with me. Eddie's around 15 now and I think he and Dad continue their visits elsewhere.

Alone on the bus the last time, I thought about how awful it was to sit there and pretend that everything was okay and I'm happy about the way things are. So I decided that I wouldn't go for any more family visits, but ever since then, I've gone back and forth on this decision. Dad had never missed a family visit, but he never fixed things so we could go back home. And now it's too late. I have to work on making my heart hard as rock, and finally, I ask Mrs. Chevalier to tell my social worker that I don't want to go for family visits anymore. I also decide that if I'm going to reject my parents, I have to reject the Chevaliers as substitute parents. From now on I have no family. I am a loner.

WHENEVER MR. CHEVALIER takes us to the zoo, he drives on Wellington Crescent so we can see all the grand houses that back onto the Assiniboine River. Some are very wide ranch-style bungalows but much larger than any in St. Norbert. I prefer contemporary houses, because we live in an old two-storey house. I try to imagine what the houses are like inside and what's in the backyards. I imagine swimming pools and tennis courts. Instead of spending money on comic books I switch to buying magazines of house plans. I spend a lot of time alone at the kitchen table, looking through them. This takes my mind off my family and I no longer think about going back home.

In church my mind wanders to house plans. While the priest is giving his sermons, I am walking around inside one of my houses and changing the rooms around. If I could sneak my magazines into church that would be perfect, but the magazines are bigger than the prayer books, so I'd get caught. At school when I'm reading a really good book, I put it inside a textbook and read, checking now and then to see where the teacher is. When I go on my own I decide I will design house plans.

IN GRADE 7 WE HAVE a grumpy old nun for our homeroom teacher and all of us are intimidated by her. I guess I must have learned from Mr. Chevalier that paper somehow comes from trees so to conserve paper I've been squeezing around 20 math calculations to a page, while others have six or nine per page. In other subjects I make my writing small, unless I want to make an answer look long.

That year the school introduces an after-school study period. I can get most of my homework done there — I'm not good at getting it done on my own. Major and Minor come to study period and Major sits right behind me. One day my teacher suddenly breaks the silence of the classroom and yells, "Béatrice Mosionier! Come up here!" At her desk I stand there while she scolds me for writing so small. How humiliating, especially since Major's there. In retaliation, I continue to write small.

In home economics class we have to make ourselves shirts. My project is going really good until I'm using the sewing machine and my finger ends up in the path of the needle. It goes right through my fingernail, down into my finger. The pain is excruciating but I remain silent because I'm so shy. I work the needle out of my finger and go to the washroom to wash the blood away. Some weeks later our teacher tells us that when we finish our shirts, we will model our clothing to the rest of the school. Needless to say, I never finish my project.

One day the boys in class leave and a teacher who isn't a nun gives us the menstruation and intercourse talk. None of this matters to me because I had started when I was nine, and I know that I am not supposed to have intercourse until I am married. Once I asked Mrs. Chevalier what tampons were because they were right beside the sanitary napkins at the drug store. She told me that good girls don't use tampons.

That year we learn that Russia, a communist country, could bomb us at any time with a hydrogen bomb. If we get a warning, we are to hide under our desks. I'm always looking out at the sky, wondering if a bomb has been dropped somewhere close. For history class I write a speech about the deficiency of totalitarianism. We have to read our speeches at the front of the class and I have challenged myself to pronounce "totalitarianism." I have a hard time pronouncing some words and I don't know why.

When I grow up I'd like to be a capitalist, but a good capitalist. I will pay good wages and be kind to those who work for me, and I will donate to charities, and everybody will be happy. I begin at home. I pay Mary from my baby-sitting money to do some of my house chores because I'm busy with more important things. When Mrs. Chevalier finds out, she puts an end to that, so I lose my first employee. I guess Mrs. Chevalier must be the government.

I started playing hooky in grade 5, but grade 6 was good, so I didn't play hooky much. Now in grade 7, I skip out on classes a lot. In past years it was mostly because I hadn't done my homework, but this year it's mostly because I don't like my teacher. Since I love reading, on days when we have library periods I never skip.

When I play hooky I walk in the woods down along the river behind the school and the cemetery. I end up at an isolated bungalow in a small clearing and I imagine living there. Trees tower overhead, creating twinkling sunlight and shade, as gentle breezes blow through the leaves. I probably imagine this house is more beautiful inside than it really is. When we go around to raise money for UNICEF, I go to all the big fancy houses, hoping to get a glimpse of what the layouts are like. I avoid the secluded bungalow because I don't want to see the inside and then be disappointed. Besides I'm too shy to go there.

At school the student council has begun work on the yearbook. Someone asks me for the spelling of my name. I want my name to take up a lot of space so I add an extra "s" and an extra "n": Beatrice Mossionnier. I hate my name anyways — it's a bad luck name — so I don't care if it is spelled wrong. At family visits it seemed that some white people would say our last name with a twinge of distaste on their faces and in their voices. I could see they looked down on my parents. Most of them were English-speaking and almost always pronounced it wrong. One of my teachers pronounced it "Monseigneur," and I was almost tempted to leave it like that.

EVERY SO OFTEN VIVIAN returns to St. Norbert to visit and I get so excited. Instead of going to Hollywood she and Kathy moved to Port Arthur, Ontario. Kathy has a daughter and it seems I'm an aunt, even though I'm only 12. Usually, when Vivian comes to the Chevaliers', Eddie comes too. One time Vivian shows us some pictures. Eddie points to one and asks, "Who's that girl with Beatrice?" Vivian and I crack up because "that girl" is Eddie when he was seven and had all that thick, curly hair. He's around 16 now and is not amused.

One time Vivian brings Kathy along. They wear high heels and make-up. Kathy is still quiet, but Vivian seems self-assured and confident, and she is still funny and still teases me. She makes me feel so special to have her as my sister. Another time she brings her boyfriend. Chuck is tall and handsome, and white. After they leave I hear that she and Chuck and Kathy have moved to Toronto.

ONE DAY EDDIE COMES to visit me. I am so honoured — it's a long walk — but I'm in my "I don't want to be seen with Natives" phase. Us foster kids never hang around together at school even though at home we work together, sing together, laugh together, and are united in believing that it's us against them. So when Eddie comes over I take him to the backyard where we talk. I don't tell him about not going to family visits anymore. I don't want him to be mad at me.

Marla and I have walked to a riding stable near King's Park. Eddie tells me he works there now and he knows all the names of the horses and which one is a good mount. He gets into a regular habit of walking to St. Norbert to visit me and soon I smarten up about being seen with other Native people. Eddie tells me tall tales. He is such a good storyteller that I believe all his stories no matter how outlandish they sound. He comes up with a plan that the three of us, Dad, me and him, will move to the Rockies, open up a riding stable, and live free. It seems that Mom left Dad a long time ago. We don't know where she is, but if she wants to come with us she could. I know that this is an impossible dream but when we talk about making it happen, we feel good.

One thing he tells me is something I already suspected. Eddie thinks Vivian is our half-sister. He thinks Mom went with a Chinese man and that's why Vivian looks part Chinese. I had always wondered about why Kathy looked like Dad, and Eddie and I looked more like Mom, but Vivian didn't look like any of us, and her skin was lighter than ours. I used to think it was because when she used to do the laundry, she would be up to her elbows in bleach water, scrubbing stains out of the whites. But that didn't explain why the rest of her was lighter.

For a while after Eddie leaves I keep thinking about it: Mom committed adultery. Adultery is a mortal sin. It's disturbing to think that my own mother would do something like that. But then I think about something else: Eddie says that Dad must have known that Vivian wasn't his but he always accepted her as his daughter. If Dad could forgive Mom, then so could I. Well, I would try. Still, *adultery?*

A HOUSING SUBDIVISION is going up on the west side of Pembina Highway, so I talk Marla and Mary into going to have a look at the houses. They are not the grand houses I've been designing but they would be more affordable. At home the four of us make a plan. When we get older, since we probably wouldn't be able to afford to buy a house on our own, we will combine our money and buy one together. And if one of us gets married, the ones left would buy that one out. Since I have no plans to ever get married, and providing they don't all get married around the same time, I figure I'll be the one left to own the house. Marla, Mary, and Melinda all say they aren't going to get married either. New plan: after we pay off one house we'll buy another one and that way we'll each get to own a house eventually.

Kathy and Vivian Mosionier, 1947

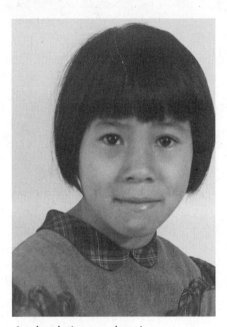

A school picture when I
was 5 years old, 1954

My sister, Vivian, at about
age sixteen, 1957

Mom & my sister, Vivian, about 1961

Me at age 14, 1963

My sister, Kathy, Mom, Chickadee, and Auntie Ada,
in Toronto, Ontario, 1964

Auntie Ada, Chickadee, John
Pranevicious and me (I'm eight
months pregnant) at the
CNE, 1967

My sister, Kathy, with her daughters, 1976

Me, Billy, Debbie and Bill, 1978

CHAPTER 7

COME AUGUST I'LL BE 13 AND in September I'll be in grade 8. I get another revelation for myself. It's the same powerful instinctive feeling that told me I had three animal guardians. I'm going to give birth to a boy; five years after that I'll have a girl; I will never be married; and I'll die when I'm 81, but I'm never really going to die. That part is confusing because everybody dies. The feeling is so powerful, but I don't quite trust it because I can't explain it. As with the animal guardians, I keep it to myself.

DURING THE SUMMER I go visit Patsy, a classmate, for a week or so. Patsy's older sister is an incredible artist. When I was younger I wanted to learn how to draw horses, so I traced them from a colouring book. Everyone gave me such compliments that I couldn't bring myself to reveal that they were traced. No one noticed that the horses in the colouring books and my horses were the same. I kept my tracings because I like horses. Now Patsy's older sister tells me my drawings are too flat and there's no life or movement to them. Compared to her drawings that's true. Ah, if only she would give me her drawings to trace.

Maybe because of my tracings I spend a week or two at an arts program at Assiniboine Park, called Painting in the Park. When the classes finish at about noon, the zoo opens and I visit the animals. Another wolf lives in the same small enclosure, is in the same pathetic condition as the previous one, and it continually paces back and forth. My other animal, the cougar, is always sleeping in the shade. The bears are the only ones who seem to have more activities to do, although sometimes one just sits there and sways back and forth, putting its weight on one front paw, then the other. I wonder if they do that in the wild or if it's a sign of insanity. Zoo visits are kind of like my family visits: first the excitement at seeing them, followed by the sadness that overshadows the visits. They should all be free and back in the wild at their real homes.

The students at this arts program are different from the kids in St. Norbert. For one thing they all like me, and they're all open and friendly, even though they must know I'm Native because I look it. They also think I'm the best artist among them. When the teacher tells us to pick a model to draw, they all want to pick me. I'm pretty sure no one in St. Norbert would pick me. It's not that all the kids in St. Norbert are mean, but it's the very few who make the most impact. Most of the St. Norbert students are really just more reserved, I think. I don't know why I see such a difference. Maybe it's because these kids didn't have to take the same Indian history we took. Or maybe it's because they don't know I'm a foster kid. Whatever the difference is, I can relax with them. We laugh and joke, just like I do with my foster sisters.

A FEW YEARS BACK, A stray collie dog that everyone calls Rover kept coming around. He looked like an old dog and he had a bald spot on his head. Everyone said not to touch him because he had ringworm. I didn't care about that. He came with me when I went walking in the woods, or he just hung around me, and he got along with all the cats.

The cat that stayed around the longest was named Kitty. Every spring she had a litter of kittens and we would try to find homes for them in the neighbourhood. She had a daughter who remained with us and we called her Mickey. She was a gentle, sweet-natured cat. She had one litter of kittens and, except for three, they all died. Then a bull mastiff that lived on the next block got loose and went on a cat-killing spree. When we found Kitty and Mickey both dead, I cried for days.

Around that time another dog was coming around. He was a big German shepherd with huge ears. I made friends with him too. One day Rover came to visit at the same time and they got into a fight. The German shepherd was hurting Rover so I jumped in to separate them. That gave Rover time to run away. He had his tail between his legs and he was yelping. Angrily I told the German shepherd I didn't want to see him again.

The next time I see him is on the morning of my thirteenth birthday when Mrs. Chevalier and I are about to go to Mass. I open the front door and there he is, but he takes off. We're walking out of the driveway when we spot Mickey's three kittens, all dead. For the rest of that day, and for days after, I cry over the dead kittens.

UNTIL GRADE 7 I HAD always taken the English-French course because it was easy. The less I challenged myself, the better. In grade 8, I forget that rule and in spite of having decided to reject the French language along with the Chevaliers as parents, I decide to take the French-French course, just to see if I can do it. Since I have a hard time pronouncing some English words, it's even harder to pronounce most French words properly; but I'm more curious about French grammar than I am about actually speaking French.

My teacher in grade 8 is also the principal of the school. Mr. Delorme introduces us to politics and he talks a great deal about U.S. President Kennedy. As I read everything I can about the Kennedy family in the *Winnipeg Tribune* and the *Winnipeg Free Press*, I discover other interesting news items. I read about Alabama and Mississippi and I'm shocked to learn how badly black people are treated down there. I've known about slavery but never thought about the origins. Now I know that white people took black people from their homes in Africa and brought them to North America. What gave them the right to do that? When I read that black people and their white supporters, civil rights workers, are killed and their murderers go unpunished, I think that we Native people have it good in Canada.

When I save enough baby-sitting money I buy a record player, 45s, and LPs. One LP has John F. Kennedy's speeches on it and every night when the lights are off I play it. I love listening to his voice. His words have such impact because he speaks so effectively about ideas that I care about. He's committed to human rights, sharing cultural and spiritual origins, helping the poor to help themselves, and he talks about freedom. This is a man who speaks the language of compassion. This is the man who established the Peace Corps. This is a man who gives hope to so many, but especially to one insignificant Native girl in St. Norbert. He makes me feel that good things are possible.

BEFORE CHRISTMAS THE SCHOOL'S Christmas choir (and that includes almost all of us) is invited to go caroling one night. One of the boys is a short, fair-haired kid who moved here a couple of years back. Some time in the next year this boy will be dead. At first kids say he was found with his throat cut, but later, the grown-ups tell us that he hung himself. I'll think about him a lot and will wonder why he would do that.

TOWARD THE END of our school year I'm thinking that Mr. Delorme is the best teacher we've had so far even though he's the strictest. For instance he's the only one who has strapped us on our hands for being late, but since I'm not the only one who's been late I don't feel singled out. I think he's the best because he has aroused my interest in events and conditions in other countries. That in turn has made me interested in learning on my own, and thinking things out.

When I was younger I used to feel sorry for myself and cry. Then I'd think of Mary and the hard times she had because of having polio. So then I'd be crying for her. Now I think of black people losing their lives or losing the ones they love and soon I'm not feeling sorry for myself anymore. I end up feeling frustrated that I can't do anything about their woes any more than I can do anything about ours. That's better than self-pity.

The Chevaliers always vote for the Liberals so I try to figure out the difference between the Liberals and the Conservatives. Partly because John A. Macdonald was a Conservative and was responsible for putting down the Métis rebellion, and mostly because the Liberals seem more balanced, and I trust the Chevaliers to make wise choices, I decide that when I get old enough to vote, I'll always vote for the Liberals.

I had been reading all these books by Albert Payson Terhune. His books are about collies like Rover and I think the first is *Lad, a Dog*. I begin to notice that whenever he needs a culprit he usually picks a black person to do the bad deed. He also doesn't seem to like mixed breed dogs and calls them curs. Although I loved his stories about collies, eventually I stop reading his books because he might be a bigot. However when a movie is made of *Lad, a Dog*, I can't resist going to see it.

St. Norbert is still growing and a new high school is built next to our school. This is where I start grade 9. Since I got only 62% in the French-French course in grade 8, I switch back to English-French. I'm lazy. I pretty much take the easy road if I have a choice.

The school splits the student body into four houses for sports. They put me in Riel House, probably because I'm Métis. I've only been trying to distance myself from this fact since grade 5. Most of the popular kids excel in sports, which is one of the reasons why they're popular. They all seem to be in Lord House. I think the idea is for the houses to compete against each other, and then the best will compete against other schools. I love most sports but not this structure and I decide not to try out for any of the sports.

We are introduced to Shakespeare and poetry and book reviews and I'm off to play hooky. Shakespeare's plays are all in old English and have nothing to do with me. I know about Pauline Johnson and I loved her poem, *The Song My Paddle Sings* (or maybe I just love the title), but other than children's verses, poetry doesn't grab my interest. And writing book reviews ruins books for me. I love reading for the pure enjoyment of it. When I was younger I'd read all the Nancy Drew books, and other detective and mystery books, and those about horses and dogs. Recently I'd gotten into biographies, mostly of well-known leaders of other countries. I don't see any good reason for writing summaries and reviews.

I now have only one A subject and that is English-French. Science, physics, math, geography, and now even English, are all beyond me. I realize now that I will never be an architect. I won't even get into university.

IN WINTERS, EVERY FRIDAY and Saturday evenings, after the rosary, we all get dressed in our winter jackets and take our skates over to the ice rink at the community centre. I love skating, even though I don't do it very well. Sometimes on the ice we hold hands all together to make a line. Some skaters go forward and some fall back and we make like a snake. I don't know who decides to do these things but I am always happy to follow along. When we get cold we warm up inside, where a fire burns in a woodstove. That is one of the few times that I love the noises of all the others as they talk — everyone seems happy — and as they change from boots to skates and thump on the wooden floor as they head for the rink. Inside, the building smells of cigarette smoke and a haze hangs over everyone.

Later when the hockey players begin putting on their gear, we know it's time to get off the ice. Sometimes we stay for a bit to watch the boys play hockey. I find the sounds of skate blades scraping the ice, and sticks slapping at the puck, mixed in with all the yells, so soothing. Sometimes at home I read a book or magazine in the living room while Mr. Chevalier watches hockey on television and I find myself dozing off. At the same time, I don't even like hockey.

MY CRUSHES ON MAJOR and Minor have finally fizzled for good. Both of them are now going with the most popular girls in school. I kind of always knew that Major and I would never go together because in his crowd boys don't go with Native girls. Knowing this made me wish I were white so many times, especially over the past three years. Some of the other boys do like me, and they're okay as friends, but if I can't have the boyfriend I want, I don't want any.

ONE OF THE BOARDERS at the convent across the street is an Indian girl "from up north." Some of the girls make fun of her and say things like,

"Don't give her food or anything, because she'll expect it all the time. That's the way 'they' are." In other words: avoid her because she's an Indian. It's not as if I have changed colour but they tell me these things as if I'm one of them. And then I make a joke about her. They all laugh and I feel accepted. But after we go our own ways I feel awful for having made the joke. So I go out of my way to walk and talk with her no matter who's around.

AT THE END OF AUGUST I catch a television news piece about Dr. Martin Luther King Jr. What really catches my attention is a part of his speech that starts with "I have a dream." There is such power in his voice, his words, himself, that I want to hear more. I want to hear the whole speech. I have no idea how to find it and, as usual, I give up.

I THINK BECAUSE Mrs. Chevalier still thinks I want to be an architect, she gets me a one-time baby-sitting job at an architect's home. When I walk into their house, I have to force myself to act nonchalant, it's so magnificent. Black marble, slate flooring, a sunken living room area, double-sided fireplace, and so much more — I can't do it justice to describe it. After the parents leave, I look in on their sleeping princess nestled in her large canopied bed and then walk around, pretending that I own the house.

That makes me think of my cardboard cutout-dolls. In this home, they would fit right in. And then it occurs to me that I would never fit in. I would enjoy designing such homes for rich people but I'm too much of a loner: I'll just need a cozy little house. On the other hand, if I were rich enough to own this house, I might be a different person than the one I am now. I might have lots of friends and I might need all this room for parties. But would I want lots of people around me? If they played baseball, that would be fun.

I keep adding details to my pretend rich life and for the rest of that evening, I'm very happy as a pretend rich person. While I'm pretending, I'm also a white person. That is what makes it all possible.

EVERYTHING SUDDENLY becomes meaningless for a few weeks because on Friday, November 22nd of that year, John F. Kennedy is shot. Sitting at my desk waiting for the final word I plead with God to let me trade places with him. Take my life; let him live. Just after 1:30 p.m., the announcement comes over the intercom that President Kennedy has died. I stand up and leave. My teacher doesn't try to stop me. Alone outside and all the way home, I cry. There I discover that Mrs. Chevalier is as shocked as I am. I didn't know she was even aware of the Kennedys.

For the rest of that weekend she and I are glued to the television. When Jack Ruby shoots Lee Harvey Oswald, I burst out, "Good!" Mrs. Chevalier replies, "It's not good. Now we'll never know what really happened." But strangely she doesn't rebuke me for approving a murder. My grief lasts for weeks. Part of my grief may be for the hope I lost.

IN EARLY DECEMBER I have a dream and I wake up crying. In my dream, Vivian is in the old outhouse in the back yard. She's sinking into all the crap down there. I am crying and pleading with her to give me her hand so I can pull her out of there. But she refuses to take my hand and she is laughing as she sinks. Years later Eddie tells me he had an eerily similar dream about Vivian, around the same time as mine.

I THINK MRS. CHEVALIER arranges for me to be with my mother over the Christmas holidays because of the way I had reacted to the Kennedy assassination. CAS had somehow found her and helped her sober up and get a job in an old folks home in Middlechurch. When I find out I have to spend time with her, I feel like a cat who has been sleeping comfortably enough by a warm fire and all of a sudden is outside in the cold. By now Mom is just any other person to me. She rejected me, I rejected her. The grown-ups think they are being kind so I don't say anything.

Mom works as a nurse's aide. I share a room with her, go with her on her rounds, and help out when I can. I never ask why she stopped coming to the family visits. Although I don't want to cause painful memories or arouse her guilt, that's not the only reason. It's not that I'm forgiving or that I'm being compassionate. It's also because the answers just don't matter any more.

The other nurse's aides are a couple of women and a man. The man thinks he's better looking than he really is and the two women think he would be a great catch. They look silly to me flirting with him and making innuendoes with sexual overtones. It's like continuing to watch a really bad soap opera just to see how disgusting it's going to get. The worst thing is that they make Mom do the really dirty work. Mom knows but doesn't complain and, often, when I offer to help, she insists on doing it herself.

One night one of the old ladies dies. While Mom cleans up around her I watch the body and wonder how they know for sure she's dead. I hope I never get so old that I have to be in an old folks home. I hate how the old people look, stuck in their chairs waiting for death. I hate the smell of this place. I hate the people who work here except for Mom. It's not that I feel close to her because I don't. I do admire that she's such a hard worker. But I can't wait to get back home. For Christmas she gives me a silly little beaded purse. I never use purses, yet I know I will keep this one for a long time, just because she gave it to me.

IN EARLY JANUARY Mrs. Chevalier receives a phone call. She's on the phone for quite a while. From the tone of her voice, it seems serious. Afterwards she calls me into her bedroom and sits me in her rocker. Right away I think I must have done something terribly wrong but I can't imagine what. Then she tells me that Vivian has died. She died in a car crash the day before. This numbs me and I just stare at Mrs. Chevalier. I had bawled my eyes out over Kennedy but the tears don't come now. Maybe I'm all cried out.

Vivian is dead. In my dream, she wanted to be dead. The dream was more real than this news of a car crash. She's gone. I'll never see her again. I try to drum up memories of her talking and laughing, memories that will bring tears but nothing comes. No memories, no tears, no reaction.

Vivian had been living in Toronto and Mom goes there to attend her funeral. Weeks later Mom sends me a letter, telling me that on January 5th, 1964, Vivian took a taxi to a pier on Lake Ontario. There she had jumped into the freezing water and drowned. Vivian had committed suicide.

CHAPTER 8

WHEN I WAS A CHILD I WORSHIPPED Vivian until she left the Chevaliers' and moved to the Tetraults'. Then I decided that since she had abandoned me she would no longer be important. But I could never keep that up because whenever I saw her she'd win my heart. She lived; I existed. She was active; I was passive. Recalling her easy, infectious laughter, I have to smile. And that's when my tears come. I cry my heart out thinking of the pain she must have had, to make her kill herself. And I wish I could have taken that pain on myself. Because now she will never, ever, bring me her special joy again.

Over the next few months I think about her suicide. I try to put myself in her place right up to the end when she must have been choking on water, to try to figure out why she felt the need to kill herself. But I don't know enough about her life in Toronto to figure out what went wrong.

IN THE SPRING I GET a letter from Kathy. She's now living in a Scarborough highrise and she asks me if I would like to come live with her in Toronto. Yes, yes, yes! Of course I want to live with her! I ask Mrs. Chevalier if I can and I think Kathy asks CAS. Mrs. Chevalier is the one who later tells me that I won't be going. She never gives me a reason and I never ask, because I know she'll have her own answers and the only answer I want is a yes. I take her no with a stony silence, but the rage I've been able to keep down rears up and stays near the surface.

Garry, a new foster boy, comes to live with us. He is bigger than me but very soft. He and Mary are in the kitchen when I hear him calling her a gimp. Mary is pretty feisty and she can usually deal with bullies on her own, but when I go in and see that she's on the verge of tears, I ask him what he just called her. He tells me it's none of my business. My rage becomes so huge that I pick him up and throw him across the room. All three of us are stunned.

I expect he will go bawling to Mrs. Chevalier but he doesn't and I am grateful. He also doesn't bully Mary again and he becomes a really nice kid. As for me, I know poor Garry stepped right into my need to release some rage. I got lucky. He could have been severely hurt. I could get into serious trouble if I can't keep my rage under control. It doesn't go away but I never physically harm anyone again.

The previous year Melinda had moved out. Without her there Marla had asked to go to St. Charles Catholic School, a convent that took in boarders, where one of her best friends was. Since I can't go live with my sister I don't want to remain at the Chevaliers. I ask to go to that convent school. I still think it is Mrs. Chevalier who decided not to let me live with Kathy although, much later, I realize it was probably Children's Aid. One way or the other, though, I'd still be moving.

That spring I get a job as a carhop at Van Buren's Restaurant, which has a drive-in section, but either I got my starting date wrong or they did. They phone for me, wondering why I've not come in. Mr. Chevalier calls me where I'm baby-sitting, arranges for one of the other kids to take over, and drives me to the restaurant. It's so good of him to do all this for me. It makes me sorry that I've decided to board at St. Charles School. He has been such a kind and fair person, and I know I will miss him a lot.

Sometimes I wish I could go back on my decision and stay, but then one of my thoughts is of graduation day. It's a big event in St. Norbert. Every graduating student has lots of family and friends who come to celebrate. I would have nobody. Well, not a real family and not real relatives. And even if I did our kind doesn't belong in St. Norbert.

At the beginning of September Mr. Chevalier loads my belongings into the back of the station wagon. Mrs. Chevalier is in the basement and I go downstairs to say goodbye. She doesn't turn around, just says goodbye. She keeps things inside, as I do, so I don't know if she's glad I'm going or if she's sad that I'm leaving. From the way she said goodbye I think she's mad. So maybe once I'm gone I will become irrelevant, much as Vivian and Mom became irrelevant to me.

On the car ride to the convent, I think about my time with the Chevaliers. I'm 15 now and I've been with them for over ten years. Three more years of school and I'll be on my own. On the whole I think I've had a good time there, thanks in part to Marla, Mary, and Melinda. It's kind of weird that I came to the Chevaliers because of Vivian, and now I'm leaving because of her.

AT THE CONVENT WE sleep in a huge dormitory with rows and rows of beds. We share a large lavatory with rows of sinks, showers, and toilet stalls, so there's not much privacy, and I have to get used to it. The nuns are quite lenient. Some of the girls put on make-up and even shave their legs. I have never heard of girls having to shave their legs. I'm still trying to figure out why anyone would spray herself with toilet water, until I learn it's some sort of perfume. But then why's it called toilet water?

What I really like about being in boarding school is that there is no cloud hanging over me about being a foster kid. I am finally just like everyone else because none of us is home. And even though I am obviously Native, it's not important to anyone here. I'm just one of many boarders.

ON WEEKENDS I STAY at Lily's place, baby-sitting for her. In the years since she left the Chevaliers' she married, has two children, and is living in the north end of Winnipeg. Eddie has turned 18 in July and is on his own. His friends, Garry and Lloyd and Lloyd's girlfriend, Diane, all live in the central area. On those weekend nights when I don't have baby-sitting to do, I walk over to Garry and Lloyd's place and usually Eddie's there. We're all Native and the humour really flies.

One night Garry and Lloyd tell me that Eddie has gotten a job way up north so he won't be coming. They go on and on, describing this new job, how he got it, and how he's going to be stuck up there for the next three months. Finally Garry says that Eddie has written to them and included a letter for me. He pulls out Eddie's letter and hands it to me. As soon as I see the paper I begin to laugh.

At that time the legal drinking age is 21. The police raid parties and arrest those who are under-age. That's how Eddie ends up in Headingley Jail on a regular basis. He only writes to me when he's in jail, and the inmates have a special legal-sized paper that they use. At first Garry and Lloyd are surprised that I know about Eddie being in Headingley, then embarrassed about the story they gave me, and finally they're laughing as much as I am. I think Eddie has given them the impression that I am an innocent, naïve Catholic girl who should be protected. I am an innocent, naïve Catholic girl but I don't need to be protected.

At first I was shocked that my brother had landed in jail but since I know he's not a bad person I don't make judgments. Eddie told me that once he was so drunk that he had trouble getting into his basement apartment, so he tried to bust a window to get in. The police arrested him and he found out he was trying to break into the wrong house.

OVER THE SUMMER HOLIDAYS CAS finds me a foster home with a weird old lady. One time she came out of the bathroom, completely naked and stood there talking to me. After that I spend as much time as I can at Lily's place. Marla has left boarding school for a foster home in Elmwood. When I'm not visiting Garry, Lloyd and Diane, or baby-sitting for Lily, I spend time with Marla and her new friends. We go for long walks and sometimes for car rides with their boyfriends.

MY SOCIAL WORKER FOR the past few years is Mrs. Simons and she's the best one yet. Some of my previous social workers came and went almost as fast as some of the summer foster kids at the Chevaliers.' Knowing that I had wanted to be an architect, one of the first things Mrs. Simons had done was to take me on a tour of the University of Manitoba. Children's Aid would have paid for my tuition and everything; but being an architect had just been a silly dream. I never even think about my house plans anymore.

While I can't play hooky at the convent my studies have not improved much. Perhaps I am writing too many letters or playing too many card games. I manage to pass grade 11, but even if I finished grade 12, I wouldn't have any skills that would get me a job in an office.

FOR THAT SUMMER I ask my worker if I can move to a boarding house. I do not want a foster home except the Chevaliers', but since I think Mrs. Chevalier was mad at me for moving, I don't ask to go to their place. My worker arranges for me to move to a downtown boarding house where many of the boarders are Native people from up north. I share a bedroom with a Native student who goes to the University of Winnipeg.

That summer I return to my restaurant job at Van Buren's. Eddie has gone to British Columbia but I still visit his friends. Some of their friends know Marla and her friends since most of us meet at the bus depot restaurant for coffee. I still baby-sit for Lily and find other baby-sitting jobs through the YWCA. I also get a monthly allowance from CAS.

One day I go visit the Chevaliers. Mary and Garry are the only foster kids there now. David and Guy are away and the house is so quiet I can hear our voices from the past. I wonder if Mr. and Mrs. Chevalier miss all our noise or if they prefer this quiet solitude. Knowing there will never again be seven children around the table makes me nostalgic. Only now do I miss the commotion.

Near the end of that summer I check out schools that have business courses. The St. Norbert and St. Charles schools only have matriculation courses: their students are supposed to go on to university or college. Since the business courses at all the vocational schools begin in grade 9, I won't be able to enroll. I will have to go to Gordon Bell High School and take grade 12 matriculation courses.

Friday and Saturday nights I go with some of my friends from the bus depot to a discotheque, the Hungry Eye, which is almost next door to the Devon Café, another of our hangouts. We can make a coffee last all night since most of our money goes into the tabletop jukeboxes. There I meet a girl named Bobbie. She has a car so we can drive wherever we want to go. And she has the most gentle dog, a black collie.

She and I get the reputation of being the "good girls," because we never drink and never "go all the way" with guys. Bobbie's crowd is mostly white but they mix easily with Native people and are friends with the crowd I know. By now I'm hanging around with a guy named Ted. He has broken up with his girlfriend, Amber, one of Bobbie's best friends, but he still misses her. I'm the shoulder he can cry on, so he's not a boyfriend, just a friend.

Some of the other boarders in my house also come to me with their problems. Even our landlady, whom I had found loud and intimidating, becomes respectful, even when I come home from all-night parties. I'm one of the few people she'll take telephone messages for. When a large front room becomes available she lets my roommate and me take it.

The all-night parties that I stay at don't really last all night. Everybody sits around and talks while drinking beer, except Bobbie and me: we only drink pop. No one ever gets drunk. At around two in the morning those who are still at the party sleep wherever they can find room. Sometimes Bobbie leaves early with a guy she really likes so that's when I stay at the party overnight. In the morning we all go to a nearby Salisbury House restaurant for breakfast and then someone drives me home.

In September I begin grade 12 at Gordon Bell High School and work at Van Buren's on weekends. At school I seem to be behind everyone else. All the classes are way more difficult than at St. Charles. I look around at the other students and wonder how come they're so smart. Or maybe I'm just getting more stupid as I get older.

The solution is to play hooky and since I'm on my own I write my own notes to the school. The last assignment I do before dropping out of school is to read *The Return of the Native* by Thomas Hardy. I'm all excited because I think it's about Native people. Then I open it up and see dialect from another country so I decide I'm not going to read it. But, because it is a school assignment, I have to. Once I get past the beginning I really like Eustacia Vye, the main character, because she reminds me of Vivian, and I can't put the book down.

In October I quit working at the restaurant, so if I'm not baby-sitting I have lots of time to meet friends for coffee. Some of them have rougher edges than Bobbie, Amber, and me. One of them, Bruno, tells me about a man who has seen me and wants to spend some time with me. He's willing to pay $300, and we could split it. I am so insulted that he would even come to me with such a proposal. With his looks and personality I had thought he was a go-getter, but not this kind of sleazy go-getter. That makes me take a closer look at some of the people we hang around with and I try to make sure I'm always with Bobbie.

In early November I drop out of Gordon Bell. Nothing has replaced my dream of being an architect. I have no ambition. I take the first job I can find, at Saan's Stores.

In the middle of November I meet Bill Culleton at a house party and we begin going out. He sort of reminds me of Sonny Bono. So far I've only had crushes on boys who have been really good-looking. It's different with Bill. I never have a crush on him, but the more time we spend together, the more he makes me feel very special. Besides being open and honest, he's independent in a way other guys are not — especially those from St. Norbert, who would never go with a Native girl. To do so would not be acceptable to their friends. Bill is safe to be with and never pressures me to go to bed with him. I'm not ready and he accepts that.

One day we're just going out, nice and safe, and the next day I'm in love with him. How did he do that? Although I don't ever want to be married, I want to be with him all the time. And then in December he tells me he has to go to Toronto and he wants me to come. Toronto — wow! That's where Kathy lives so of course I want to go. At this time I don't know where my parents live, where Eddie lives, or where Kathy lives. I only know that once I get to Toronto, I can find her.

Later that month Bill leaves so he can find a job and a place for us to live and I give two weeks notice to Saan's Stores. I go see Mrs. Simons, my social worker, to let her know I'm going to Toronto. She asks if there is anything she can say to make me change my mind. I smile and say no. I may only be 17 but I know what I want.

What I don't know is that I will be seeing her again in less than a year.

part two

A Lonely
Walk
Home

JANUARY 1967 TO
OCTOBER 1980

INTERVIEW PART TWO

I STARTED WORKING OUT. I went right to Alberta. And from there, I got a job cooking for the stone diggers, in Saskatchewan and in Alberta. Yeah. And then I had a job on the waterland district, to go and cook for the men over there. And I worked there for quite a while. And then after, I came back to my husband.

The Children's Aid used to bring them in a place. And it's very hard when you go visit your children and then they have to go away again. We used to cry lots of times. My little son, I remember one time I went to visit him, and I took him home with me and he stayed with us. My husband was with me that time. And, uh, I was supposed to bring him back that Sunday. And I couldn't. And then, yeah, Sunday, Monday, Tuesday, Wednesday, Thursday, I brought him back. He just hung on to me. That's very hard. [She is weeping.]

And then you think of God. Why did this thing happen to me?

I can't say no more.

I heard him, I heard him crying, when they come and grab him. It's hard for a mother to see those things. But I am a Roman Catholic. And I believe in God. And I believe in the Blessed Virgin Mary. She suffered too. She seen her son being crucified. And that's the one I used to think about. And that way, my sorrows eased up a little bit.

Oh, I had a tough time, when I was young too. But, there is a God up in heaven. He will understand and He will take you home with Him.

They [Children's Aid] didn't tell me where they were. Vivian and Kathy, they put them, uh, in different places. But Kathy was the one that used to run away from where they put her at. She must have been about 16, going on 17. And then I used to hide her. Sometimes I had her for a month. Hiding her, eh. Sure they were looking for her but I used to go hide her. Sometimes even the big detectives were looking for her.

And that's when they come and found her. When we were, um, we were staying on Jarvis. Yeah, two great big detectives came and got her from there. I don't know how they knew. But I was never scared of them, to talk to them. And they told me, "We have to do that. Our duty." They come and get her. Kathy was the only one that ran away, lots of times. She was lonesome. She, I guess she didn't like it there, eh. And then I would take her. One time I took her to Selkirk, Manitoba. Nobody ever knew where she was.

But I couldn't get along with my husband. So I had to leave him again. But every time, when the job was on, I used to go out to the waterland district to go and cook for the bushmen. Yeah. I was getting $75 a month. And that's when they released Kathy. She come out and stayed with me out there. Uh, she was staying with a fellow here. She had a little girl, eh. With that guy. And, uh, I looked after my grandchild, Kathy's little girl. She was just crawling then, that time. And Kathy and that guy she was living with, they were working in Winnipeg, and I looked after their little baby out there. They'd come and see her, eh. Saturday, they'd come, and sleeping over. And those were my happiest days when I seen my little grandchild. And after, they moved away.

Vivian already was married that time. And they used to come and stay at my place. They used to come to wherever I was. Oh, that's one thing I'll say with my two girls. They used to come and find me.

I went in Duck Bay. I got a half-brother out there. Pat Pelletier. I stayed in Duck Bay pretty near five year. I had a little house out there, by myself. I didn't have nobody to . . . just myself. I got along pretty good out there. I used to make cabbage rolls, and I used to sell them. I bake bread and I used to sell my bread. Over there, I was never broke.

And then I got relief here in Winnipeg but you have to be . . . when you get money from there, eh, you got to see that every penny wasn't wasted. You had to buy what you have to buy. Of course, I buy sometimes, beer, for, with my friends. Already that was in my system, I guess. Oh, I uh, I drink. Once in a while, I drink, sure. Yeah.

— *MARY CLARA PELLETIER MOSIONIER*

CHAPTER 9

ON THE TRAIN RIDE TO TORONTO I meet an older lady and a young couple. We play cards and joke around and laugh almost all the way to Toronto. But in my quiet times alone I ponder the decision I've made. Although the values of being a good Catholic girl were instilled in me daily, here I am on my way to live with a man with no intention of marrying him.

For the past six months I've sort of been part of a group very different from the people with whom I was raised. I say "sort of" because I've been more on the fringe. I don't drink beer and I don't fool around, and until that Bruno approached me with his stupid proposal — I still bristle at that — I hadn't thought this was a wild bunch. I hadn't seen anyone drunk and I hadn't seen any fights. Yeah, a few of the Native girls who I knew and liked had done time for drinking under the age of 21 or for shoplifting. But on the whole, to use Bobbie's expression, "they were good people."

From this group, my heart — and not my brain — has chosen a man. Any of the boys from St. Norbert, the good Catholic boys I might have wanted, would not have had the guts to go with me. They were stuck where I had been in my 'I don't want to be seen with other Natives' days — where I might still be if not for my brother.

Just because I'll be living with Bill doesn't mean I have to lose my virginity. I think one of the reasons why he makes me feel special is that he respects me. There seems to be an innocence about me that makes people, some who are almost strangers, want to protect me.

For example, recently at the Devon Café, a couple of really tough women told me another woman had threatened to come after me because her boyfriend had apparently looked at me with interest. Although we didn't know each other, these two tough women took it on themselves to protect me by telling this other one that if she wanted to get at me, she'd have to go through them first.

Bill is on night shift so he can't meet me at the train station; but he has a friend who will meet me at the furnished flat he rented for us. When I left Winnipeg, it felt like a hundred below with snow three feet high. When I walk out of the Toronto train station, the night air is filled with a fine mist, there's no snow, and it's not at all cold. I fall in love with Toronto immediately.

Those first few weeks are wonderful and my positive outlook is probably what gets me the first job I apply for, as a store clerk in the hardware department at a nearby Woolworth's store. Bill's brother, Ryan, and his wife, Anita, live nearby. Right away I become good friends with Anita and we often visit them.

Living with a man isn't much different from living in a dormitory full of girls, except that I sleep in the same bed as him. In the middle of January I give up my virginity. If I'm never going to get married, I can't stay a virgin all my life, can I? Bill wants to give me an engagement ring but I never liked diamonds or gold and I tell him no.

ONE EVENING AFTER SUPPER I take a streetcar to the address on Kathy's most recent letter. Someone else lives there, but I knock on nearby doors and ask if they know Kathy Mosionier. Finally one lady says yes and even has Kathy's phone number. When I call, an older woman answers. She tells me she's my Auntie Ada. I've never heard of her before. She tells me Kathy works the night shift at the post office and invites me over. I tell her I'll come over earlier the next evening, when Kathy's there.

The last time I saw Kathy was when Vivian brought her to St. Norbert for a brief visit; but the next evening as we stand face to face, the excitement I used to have at early family visits is not there. We are strangers. Because we are sisters, we hug; but she is as reserved as I am. I meet her boyfriend, Larry Blais, and her three-year-old daughter, nicknamed Chickadee. They live with Ada and her husband, John Pranevicious.

AT THE END OF FEBRUARY I realize that I have missed my period. Could you really get pregnant after one time? I didn't even enjoy it. It hurt like hell and I didn't want to do it again. What if I am pregnant? No, I couldn't be. But what if I am? What am I going to do? At first I keep my suspicion to myself, but at the end of March, I finally tell Bill. He doesn't react, so I think everything will be okay.

OVER THE NEXT FEW MONTHS when I visit in the evenings, Kathy and I go out for coffee at a restaurant before she heads downtown to work. One night instead of going to work she sleeps over at my place. I'm always conscious that she's my older sister though we never get close enough to joke around. When she does laugh, it's a beautiful sound and reminds me of Dad's laugh, but I sense that she's not happy. Maybe she doesn't like her job. Larry doesn't seem to work and he's bossy. Some evenings it seems like he's hurrying her off to work.

One evening when I get there Kathy and Larry are quarrelling. Then he threatens that he's going to tell me. Tell me what, I wonder. The threat makes Kathy quit arguing and she begs him not to. She'll go to work right now but please don't tell her.

He turns to me and says, "She turns tricks. That's what she does for a living."

I am shocked but I don't feel disappointed in Kathy. I get angry with Larry. He's the one who sends her out there and he's probably living off the money she makes. I don't tell him what I think of him, that he's a self-absorbed asshole, because he might take it out on Kathy.

NOW I HAVE TWO PROBLEMS: Kathy's work and my pregnancy. Soon I have a third, one that makes me stop thinking about Kathy's problem. I come home from work to find that all of Bill's things are gone. We didn't even have an argument. I feel as if he took a knife and sliced my heart in half. For weeks, I'm heartbroken, empty except for self-pity, until gradually there's nothing inside me but a dull ache.

When I do let myself think of him, it's not of the cold abrupt way he left me. It's of the good times we had together: going out to movies and dinners, holding hands, talking, laughing, watching TV, going grocery shopping. I miss lying in his arms at night, his gentleness and patience with me. I miss how he made me feel safe, sort of like how I used to feel when I would climb into the safety of Vivian's bed when I was little.

I don't dwell on those times when he was out late at night. While I would get home by ten after visits with Kathy, he would come in after midnight. Although I knew he was out with the friends he had from his previous visits to Toronto, I would later get angry about his late nights. I never imagined him with someone else because he had convinced me that he loved me.

Even though he's gone, I still believe he loves me and he'll never stop loving me. I'm so certain that Bill will come back that the dull ache fades away. I settle in to wait for his return. I've had the best of training in the ways of waiting.

AT WORK I CONFIDE IN my only friend that I'm pregnant and that Bill left me. Right away, Frances says I can share her place, which is fortunate, because I can't afford my flat on my own.

One morning we're walking to work and we encounter a mother pushing her baby in a carriage. Right away Frances makes a fuss over the baby, while I stand back and watch. Afterward Frances shakes her head at me and says, "Beatrice, you'll never make a good mother."

If I don't make a good mother, it's not because I don't fuss over other peoples' babies. It'll be because I have no idea how to be a mother.

I NEED TO SAVE MONEY for when my baby is born so, for entertainment, I spend a lot of time reading books from the public library. Whoever thought up public libraries is the best. I've learned that pregnant women have to have prenatal care so I've secretly been attending to that at St. Michael's outpatient. For the first five, six months I don't show at all, although I've gained a bit of weight from my usual 108 pounds. If the doctors didn't keep seeing me I wouldn't even think I was pregnant. I might be able to work right up until delivery time.

Frances has been very good about keeping my secret and covering for me when I have to go for my checkups. It's me who has a big mouth. I accidentally let it slip to one of the other clerks, telling her about all the things I'm going to buy for my baby. She tells the supervisor, who gives me my two-week notice — plenty of time for all the clerks, except Frances, to look down on me for being an unwed mother. To be.

EVEN WITHOUT BILL, I remain good friends with his sister-in-law, Anita. When she met Bill's brother, Ryan, she spoke only French and he spoke only English; yet they still got together and are married. Now Anita's sister from Montreal, Denise, is staying with them. Like me, Denise is pregnant and her boyfriend left her. We also become very good friends. These friends and Kathy and Auntie Ada help me pass the time as I wait for Bill.

AFTER LOSING MY JOB I consider going on welfare but don't know how to do that and I don't really want to be on welfare, so I find a job as a mother's helper. The lady who hires me lives way out in the suburbs. She has two children who are four and six, and a baby. I clean, do the ironing, take her children for walks, and baby-sit when needed. Her baby starts calling me Bee-ah, and I think she's pronouncing the "a" in Bea. It doesn't occur to me until years later that she's just a baby, and doesn't even know how to spell.

In the middle of August Denise gives birth to a baby girl and asks me to arrange for the baptism at a neighbourhood church. The Sunday bus trip from the suburbs takes so long that by the time I get to the church no one is there. At the rectory the priest agrees to perform the baptism if I can bring back the mother and baby. Denise was very upset that I hadn't shown up but is really happy with the alternate arrangement. Shortly after that day she returns to Montreal with her daughter. It will be years before I see her again.

At the end of August Kathy and I decide to celebrate our birthdays by going to the Ex (Canadian National Exhibition) with Chickadee, Auntie Ada, and John. Larry is not invited and we have a great time. I return to my mother's helper job, not knowing that I won't be seeing Kathy and Chickadee for a very long time.

BILL WRITES TO ME, just as I knew he would. After we exchange a few letters he asks me to join him in Winnipeg. I'm elated. I can hardly wait to see him again and be back where I belong — in his arms. The other thought is that our baby will need a father and now that's going to happen. I give notice, pack, and by the middle of September I'm back in Winnipeg.

Bill is not at the train station to meet me, even though I've written him, giving my arrival time. I wait until the station is almost empty, positive that he will show up. Maybe he got the day wrong. Maybe I wrote down the wrong day. Maybe he came yesterday and thinks I'm the one who chose not to show up. Well, I'm here so what do I do now? I go to the return address on his last letter to me. No one is there. I go to a North End Salisbury House restaurant where we used to go for breakfasts, then back to the train station and to downtown Salisbury House restaurants, hoping to run into him or someone we know. Without him, Winnipeg is almost like a foreign city, cold and uncaring. I feel so lost and alone. I can't let myself cry in front of all the strangers on the street.

By the end of that first day I take a room for the week in a downtown rooming house and the first thing I do is to sit on the sofa bed and cry my heart out. Why did he do this to me? Why get me to come out here? Why not just leave me be? I can't believe I was so wrong about him. And again I wonder, "What will I do now?"

THE NEXT DAY I go to the bus depot and the Devon Café, and it's as if all the people I had known before had disappeared. I don't want to see Garry, Lloyd, or Diane, because I'm now obviously pregnant and ashamed. To pass the time, the one place I can go to for free is to the library.

By the end of September I'm whipped, defeated, and I'm also broke.

If I didn't need rent money, I would delay the phone call that I now have to make. I call Mrs. Simons, my last social worker, tell her that I'm pregnant and have no money. I don't tell her about Bill. She makes no judgment, just says she'll meet me right away. When we meet, she asks if I would like to go to a home for unwed mothers. I nod.

She drives me to the Villa Rosa, a few blocks from the Misericordia Hospital. When I'm being registered, the nun tells me that each girl is given a name that begins with the first letter of her last name: They offer me 'Mildred.' At another time I would have preferred Mariah, like in *They Call the Wind Mariah*. But I'm beyond caring. Nothing matters now.

I'm the only Native girl but the other girls are nice and a few seem determined to cheer the rest of us up. And for the most part they succeed. I discover an ability to live 'in the now,' and to leave the traumas of the past in the past. This requires a lot of concentration, as does learning to relax to make birthing easier.

We all have chores to do. The light chores are given to those who are due soon, and as everyone thinks I'm due in November or December, my job is to wash floors. In early October in the afternoon, my contractions begin, and at 4:30 p.m., a surprised nun walks with me to the Misericordia Hospital. At 6:00 p.m. the doctor says, "I hope you wanted a son."

Until this second I had wanted a daughter but I am ecstatic. "Yes," I say, "Yes. I did want a son."

CHAPTER 10

MY SON LOOKS PERFECT, NOT CRINKLED and mottled like some. He's perfectly proportioned and takes after his father, with fair skin and brown hair. He looks so healthy — and it will be up to me to keep him that way. It's as if God gave me a perfect baby to make up for all the bad times I had, even though they were usually due to my mistakes. I promise Him that I will be such a good mother that He will be proud of me. Distant memories of my guardian animals stir in me and I think that I could learn from them by following my maternal instincts.

As soon as I'm able, I phone Denise in Montreal and we're both very emotional. She tells me that Anita and Ryan have moved to Winnipeg and gives me their address. Anita is due to give birth in January.

Mrs. Simons finds a room for us on the second floor of a family-owned house. I spend the next six weeks with my son, going out only to get food or to take him to the doctor's. My landlady lets me do the laundry in the basement. In return I sometimes baby-sit for her.

Billy is a happy, sociable baby. He never cries because I'm always there to feed or change him. Sometimes I wake up during the night just to look at him. He lies on his back, his eyes open, almost as if he's deep in thought. Sometimes I have dreams that he's talking with me, even though he's just a baby. These few months are one of the most relaxed, contented times of my life.

The landlord and landlady urge me to go out and visit someone. They joke that I might forget what grown-up people look like. I finally visit Garry, Lloyd, and Diane and they tell me Eddie is back in town. In an old building off Main Street, I climb the stairs to his third-floor apartment. An older man passes me on his way down, a cap hiding his face. A weird sensation comes over me. At the top I stare back down at the man. "Dad?"

He looks up. Sure enough, it's Dad!

He lives up on the fourth floor and had no idea that Eddie also lives in the building. We end up having a family reunion, although no one knows where Mom is.

Driven by superstition rather than belief, I felt a need to have Billy baptized. I had already written to Anita, who's agreed to be Billy's godmother, and now Eddie agrees to be the godfather. Later I'll make the arrangements at Our Lady of Fatima Church and Billy will be baptized in early December.

THROUGH ANITA, BILL and I get in touch again. He writes, asking me to return to Toronto. In spite of trying to be hard-hearted toward him, my initial reaction from reading his letter is pure joy. I temper that joy by convincing myself that with or without him, I do want to go back to Toronto. Kathy and Auntie Ada are both there and I miss them. With Eddie planning to return to British Columbia, there would be no one here for me. I write to Bill and because I now believe I can live without him and have nothing to lose, I tell him he'll have to send train fare. I don't expect an answer, considering what he did in September. Or what he didn't do.

At the end of November, I get a job. Although Children's Aid gives me money and I don't really need to work, I feel a need to regain a sense of independence. I need to rebuild my savings. Because it's pre-Christmas, I get a three-week job at Eaton's, but I get fired for making a clerical mistake. That's embarrassing, but I miss Billy so much when I am at work, I decide to stay home until after Christmas.

Not only does Bill reply to my letter, but he sends more than enough for the train fare. I pack, book a train compartment, and once again say goodbye to Mrs. Simons. The train attendant is really nice. He warms up Billy's bottles of milk, brings my food to me, and helps out any way he can.

BY THE END OF December 1967 I'm back in Toronto living 'in the now,' just happy to be with Bill. We can't afford a crib for Billy so two big armchairs facing each other become his bed. At the laundromat I run into Florence, a lady I had met at the first place Bill and I had rented. Now she's a stay-at-home mom of a little boy and lives a couple of blocks away. She agrees to baby-sit Billy, and I get a sorting job at a nearby commercial laundry for a dollar an hour.

After a couple of months Bill leaves again. I'm devastated, but I have a baby to look after and need to find a place I can afford. Florence tells me there's a room for rent next to their flat, and I move in. Billy has to sleep in my bed on the wall side.

I LEAVE THE LAUNDRY for a job inspecting watchbands made in a factory — fewer strangers' germs but the money is no better. There, I make friends with two girls from Quebec and with another inspector. She's having a long-term affair with a married man so she's usually depressed. I like her but her adulterous affair unsettles me. Most of the other workers are Italian women.

After many months of saving I buy a stroller and one evening I'm out walking Billy with my friend, when we encounter a group from work. One of the women calls Billy a bastard. This hurts so much I can't talk, but my friend, who is already feuding with them sure can — and does. At work others ridicule me for being an unwed mother until the supervisor steps in. I don't know what she says but everyone suddenly becomes super nice.

MAKING SURE THAT Billy is well clothed and fed, and buying the extra things for him doesn't leave much money. A bakery I pass on my way to work sells cheap broken cookies, and once in a while my baby-sitter invites me to supper. When I take Billy out for walks we sometimes pass a restaurant: the smells make my mouth water and my stomach rumble. French fries and a hamburger would be heavenly.

My friends from Quebec leave but another girl takes their place, becoming a close friend. Wanda has an expression I will use again and again to cheer myself up: "Better days are coming." That is until I realize I should have been saying, "Good days are here now."

Wanda tells me where the closest library is and I soon come across books about positive thinking, by Andrew Carnegie and Napoleon Hill. I try to incorporate their ideas into my daily living, although it's hard to remember all the specifics. One of the exercises is to write out a list of everything I like about myself on the left side and the things I don't like on the right side. On the left, I list that I'm compassionate, fair, just, considerate of others' feelings, thoughtful, non-judgmental, trustworthy, resilient, friendly, naturally shy, humble, loyal, patient, stubborn in a good way, trusting, and independent — except for Bill.

What I don't like is that I'm lazy. That goes at the top of the list on the right. I fear criticism; I'm sometimes vain; I'm a procrastinator; I have no self-discipline; I lack persistence; I allow others to take control (Bill again); I compromise too easily; I'm always wishing instead of willing something good to happen; I'm reactive, which makes me subject to others' moods; and I'm negative in feeling that because I'm Native, I can't be or do the things I want. I lack long-term ambition; I'm uneducated; I'm poor; I still have Catholic superstitions, and I'm indecisive. So maybe I'm not so independent.

What I'm supposed to do with this list is strengthen the qualities I like and get rid of the ones I don't like. I don't have a desire to make lots of money and even if I did I wouldn't know how to go about it. I just want to be able to support my son and be a better person, because it should follow that if I become a better person, then I'd be a good mother.

I sometimes still hang out with Bill's crowd and I begin going with Matt, but we never get serious, because he's aware that my thoughts are always of Bill. Matt is the most reliable, steady person I know. He would make a great husband and father, but I don't fall in love with him. Eventually he begins going with another woman, although we remain good friends. By going with him, I had tried to exorcise Bill. Unfortunately, it didn't work. For me to put Bill out of my life completely, he would have to marry someone else.

Kathy and Chickadee moved away from Auntie Ada's apartment while I was in Winnipeg and didn't leave an address or phone number. Auntie Ada tells me that Larry left Kathy and married someone else. Since she is my connection to Kathy, I don't want to lose track of her, so I visit as often as I can.

IN THE SPRING OF 1969 Bill returns and I'm on 'cloud ten', I'm that happy. He rents a duplex for $85 a month and by renting the upstairs flat to one of his friends for $20 a week, we have no problems paying the rent. The house is far from my work and when I give notice, the supervisor tells me I'm eligible for unemployment insurance. I apply and look for a job within walking distance.

One day there's a knock on the door. It's Eddie, my brother, who has found me through Auntie Ada. I'm ecstatic to see him. He has a wife and her three children with him and he wants to find a job and stay awhile. We go together to look for jobs, but neither of us finds one.

As we talk about the past he tells me he was disappointed in Vivian, Kathy and me, because he saw us as "apples": red on the outside and white on the inside. While I resent this, I can't argue with it; here I am living with a white man, surrounded by white people, whereas he's spent time on different reserves in British Columbia and has taken the time to learn more about Indian people. Our talks create a chasm between us — not wanting to hurt his feelings, I don't tell him that I prefer my lifestyle to his. About a week or two later, Eddie decides they'll go back to Winnipeg, or maybe back to Vancouver. I'll miss him. At the same time, I'm relieved that I won't have to bear his disappointment in me firsthand.

After he leaves I learn that the unemployment office could upgrade me to a clerical position and they would pay my living expenses plus tuition for a ten-month course. I jump at that chance, choosing a bookkeeping component over secretarial, because at all my previous jobs the bookkeepers were men. If they could support their families with book-keeping, then that's what I want. I can't believe my luck when I begin at George Brown College. In a short refresher course, I suddenly understand math like I never did in high school. It's as if something in my brain has been unplugged allowing some mathematical intelligence out.

EVEN THOUGH IT'S BEEN about a year since that woman called my son a bastard, and even though she became nice to me, that word sticks in my mind. I decide Bill and I should get married and in May 1969, we do, at city hall. It's not confetti, flowers, and wedding bands — the witness is a stranger from one of the other marriage parties. We do love each other but because I never wanted to get married, I tell myself the marriage is just so that no one will ever call my son a bastard again.

WE SPEND THE MONEY we have saved from renting out the upstairs apartment on a tent and fishing gear, and go camping up north. We like that so much, we think of buying a cottage lot. We find one north of the Severn River, and the salesman tells us we can camp up there that weekend. It's perfect. The whole area is undeveloped — not a car or a person in sight. After setting up the tent, Bill goes back to town to rent a boat. Billy and I stay at the campsite. When it gets dark, although I'm not afraid to be alone in the woods with my child, I can't figure out how Bill is going to find us. I make a fire to cook our supper and that's how Bill finds our campsite from the river.

Bill tells his friends about the place and they all want to come. We end up renting it for the month and about a dozen of us camp there. There's no drinking, or anything like that. Most of the guys go fishing during the day, and Billy and I go along with Bill. My favourite times are lying across the widest seat, reading or napping or listening to Bill and Billy talk as they troll for fish. At night there's a huge fish fry and after supper we sit around the fire. Those weekends make everything I've been through with Bill worthwhile. Billy is enthralled with his father and is as happy as I am.

Our landlord sells our house to a developer and we have to move out. Bill finds a small basement apartment in the suburbs. The Italian landlady upstairs baby-sits for me. It isn't long before we notice that Billy waves his arms about as he babbles to us. Then we realize we will soon have a fluent Italian-speaking toddler.

In October Bill leaves again and this time I know without a doubt that another woman is involved. Until now I'd had this dumb idea that when he left me, he was abstaining from sex, because he had allowed me to remain a virgin until I was ready. After our ideal summer and seeing what was possible, I am all the more devastated by his betrayal. My heart isn't cut in half this time; it's all in little pieces and it will never heal.

The next day at school I must look the way I feel. In the hall George Moehring, a friend in my class, asks me what's wrong. Instead of answering, I start bawling and bury my face against his shoulder because I don't want anyone to see me crying. He takes me for a drive and I tell him what has happened.

George has an idea but he doesn't tell me about it. He is president of our campus, and elections for student council are underway. He nominates me for member-at-large and the students have such a high regard for him that they elect me to the student council. His plan works because now that I'm on the council, I'm involved with school activities and that takes my mind off Bill.

Once again I have to move because, as usual, I can't afford the rent on my own. Therese, another school friend, invites me to share a flat with her and another French girl. When Auntie Ada agrees to take Billy during the week, I accept.

George is an amazing guy. He really seems to care about other people. For example, the vice-principal wants all the girls to wear office clothes, as if we are in a real office environment. George explains to him that students can't afford office clothes, because most of us are barely getting by. When the vice-principal refuses to budge, George goes to the principal and the rule is rescinded. George also solves a problem with our book-keeping teacher. He was so intimidating and sarcastic that most of us are too scared to ask questions. George takes most of the class along to air our concerns to the principal. The principal has a talk with our teacher who becomes much nicer. I had a really hard time understanding book-keeping, and George takes the time to explain things and finally, it clicks into place.

George reminds me of a lion: he's tall, has thick tawny-brownish hair and great presence. Oh, and he also has a pride of lionesses. At first I'm immune because I want to be with Bill. Then I find that I'm watching for him to come to class, or to walk into the cafeteria where he joins our group. Whoa! I need to keep myself in check: he has a bit of the scoundrel in him and he is definitely not a one-woman man. Besides, even though I'm separated, I am married.

THE STUDENT COUNCILS from the five campuses meet once a month to plan the finances and big events. I'm assigned to help the photographer and his assistant schedule the students at our campus to have their pictures taken. That means going to each classroom and talking to the teachers and students. What if some of the teachers don't take kindly to me disrupting their classes? I send out advance notices and all the teachers are fine when I walk into their classrooms.

Next I have to talk over the microphone in the cafeteria to hundreds of students. It's my job to tell them about coming events that the student council has planned. I never dreamed I would or could do such a thing. The first time George and Therese try to reassure me, but before I go up to the mike to make the announcements, my stomach is in knots. I concentrate really hard on getting the message across. Then I discover that I like my voice being spread throughout the cafeteria — having a job to do overcomes my shyness. Many of the students seem to like me — or maybe it's the message. Either way, I must come across okay. After that, speaking publicly at my campus isn't so bad.

At the monthly meetings of all five student councils, it's a different story. Since I don't have anything specific to say, I rarely speak up. After those meetings I sometimes go along to the parties or dance clubs or even to the pubs. Because I'm under 21, I never drink alcohol. That's illegal and I could go to jail.

I do try marijuana a couple of times. It's the hippie era and I go with Therese and a few others to Yorkville a couple of times, where kids openly smoke joints — it doesn't seem to be illegal — and the night air is filled with that sweet but pungent odour, as we make our way through the crowds, looking for a coffeehouse. I prefer the free-spirited hippies to the conformists like me because they don't care what the conformists think of them. I would like to be like that. So when I'm at a couple of house parties I give pot a try, but I don't like it much, so I quit.

Fridays after school I head over to my aunt's to be with Billy for the weekend. Sometimes I feel really guilty for not spending all my free time with him. And if I wasn't involved in all the school activities, I'd have more free time. Then on the other hand, I think I'm where I need to be, doing what I need to do.

Looking back, as the course finishes, I find that I've been part of many activities with many different people — and for the first time in my life, I feel I've taken part in a leadership role, despite my shyness. When our course finishes in February 1970 my roommates return to Quebec and my unemployment insurance stops. Now I need to find a job quickly, but a better-paying one this time, so Billy and I won't be so poor.

CHAPTER 11

SINCE I LACK THE SELF-CONFIDENCE to send out a resume with no
previous experience as a bookkeeper, I sign up with a temp agency. My luck is definitely changing. I've found a place to rent where the
landlady agrees to baby-sit Billy. The upstairs apartment has no door,
just stairs that go up to a landing and hallway, and I have a kitchen,
living room, a bedroom, and a bathroom. On my third assignment the temp agency sends me to Wahn, Mayer & Smith, a large
downtown law firm. They hire me permanently and I work in the
accounting office with four others, supervised by the comptroller. On
my own I would never have had the audacity to apply for a job in a
place like this.

I really love working at this law firm. Everybody seems to be func-
tional, while my life with Bill has been completely dysfunctional. Secretaries talk about their plans to ski on winter weekends, or go to the
cottage on summer weekends. They talk about vacation plans to exotic
destinations. They talk about redecorating their homes or what car
they'll buy. And they talk about their families, past and present. I have
nothing to talk about. I just listen.

Sometimes the secretaries get together at one of their places, usually
for bridal or baby showers. The father of one of the accounting clerks
owns a huge construction company, millionaire stuff. And the comp-

troller's secretary has us over to her mansion. It seems to me that everybody there is super-rich, super-beautiful, or super-smart. I am none of these things but I admire most everyone around me for their abilities. My co-workers in accounting know of my personal situation and they never make me feel like I'm lower class. It seems that I'm the only one acutely aware of being an economic outsider.

At lunch we either go to nearby restaurants or have our lunches delivered and play cards in the lunchroom. I enjoy the games but I'm still very shy. A simple question could make my face flush. The confidence I found at George Brown College has melted away and I've reverted to my usual tongue-tied self, unless something is important to me. When I first arrive, the accounting staff has to walk to the other end of the building for coffee. I would buy milk for my coffee and by lunchtime it was usually gone, so I talk my boss into getting us a small fridge and coffeemaker near our department. Such a small thing but for me it's a huge accomplishment.

A FEW TIMES GEORGE and I meet for supper. He has two daughters and a son but has been divorced for many years. He's moving to Hamilton in September to attend McMaster University. I figure I will never see him again. I'll certainly never forget him and I will miss him, a lot. I'm 20 and I won't see him again until I'm 38.

IN SUMMER I TAKE Billy out for long walks in the stroller, stopping at a couple of the parks along the way, or we go do laundry. When we go somewhere by streetcar, we don't take the stroller. One time Billy and I are walking hand in hand. I am thinking about something and not paying attention. Suddenly Billy pulls me back from crossing a laneway, and as I look down at him to see why, a car whizzes by. I am wonderstruck by my three-year-old son. I'm again filled with gratitude for having him. Without him, what would my life be like? Might I have gotten into drinking, or drugs, or partying all the time?

Although it takes two to make a child, my gratitude doesn't extend to Bill. I decide to divorce him. A law clerk in the firm is assigned to my case. As I tell him the details of my marriage, it occurs to me that I must sound like an idiot. Thankfully, he doesn't seem to judge me for having such a screwed-up life.

Bill comes to see me and asks me to go back to Winnipeg with him. At first I want to be snide and ask him what happened with his girlfriend, but something better comes to mind. I tell him sure, go rent a house, and then Billy and I will come. He agrees and some time later, writes to say that everything is ready. I have no intention of giving up my job to go into an unknown situation in Winnipeg. All I want is revenge. But on the day that he's expecting me, revenge doesn't feel so good. I feel sorry and guilty that we're not going to show up. All that day I keep reminding myself of all he put me through but that doesn't help much. Revenge is not for me.

When Bill returns to Toronto he still wants to reconcile. I'm reluctant to go back with him. However my feelings of sorrow and guilt are aroused, so I compromise by dropping the divorce proceedings. Then he has a new proposal: let's buy a place of our own. Okay, that does it — we'd never have to move again.

We buy a condo in Mississauga and I buy a car. One of Bill's friends teaches me how to drive. To get to work I drive to downtown Toronto, park on a side street, and walk the rest of the way. This stresses me out since I only have a beginner's license — I shouldn't be driving alone — and gas takes a big chunk out of my pay. I've been getting regular pay raises, but when I ask for one and they turn me down I give my notice. I find a bookkeeping job in a small Mississauga law firm within easy driving distance.

One morning on my way to work I'm very low on gas and just before I can reach the gas station, my car stalls. A police officer pulls up right behind me. He gets in my car, which becomes as intimidated as I am, and the officer starts it immediately. He drives my car onto the shoulder, a garage attendant brings me some gas, and I'm off to work. That was too close so I put off paying other bills in favour of professional driving lessons. Then after failing once, I get my license.

No surprise, in March Bill leaves again. I know I should just let him go and be done with him. I just can't make myself change. He's part of me just as Billy is part of me.

Shortly after my son was born I bought a life insurance policy with Billy as beneficiary. The insurance broker, Mr. Resnick, was an older man with a deep, kind, gravelly voice. Over the years I've been able to tell him about my life and he's been almost like a substitute father to me. He is never judgmental so I can be totally honest. Because of Mr. Resnick's kindness, and because he's one of those people who made me feel good about myself, if only for a little while, I have always kept up the insurance premiums.

Unfortunately, I can't keep up the mortgage payments and the condo fees. I sell off what furniture I can and give the rest to Leslie, another single mother. Not knowing that I could put the condo up for sale, even though we had a closed mortgage, I just walk away from it.

That summer Bill is back and I'm about seven months pregnant. He has a new plan. I'm a grown-up — I could have and should have said no to him and his plan, but I don't. So after a brief stay in Calgary we end up back in Winnipeg. Bill gets us a ground-floor apartment with a door that opens to a back courtyard where the children play. I had applied for unemployment insurance in Calgary, but because we moved, I hadn't received any cheques. I make sure the Winnipeg office has my new address. Bill finds odd jobs here and there, barely making enough for food and rent.

I become friends with Tanya, who is married to Don, one of Bill's friends. At the beginning of the hunting season Bill and Don go deer hunting to stock up on meat for the winter. Billy and I stay with Tanya. One morning I wake up to find my water has broken and Tanya calls the police to take me to the hospital. They seem to be in no hurry although I'm in the back seat timing my contractions. About an hour after I get to the hospital, I give birth to my daughter.

CHAPTER 12

I'VE ALWAYS WANTED A DAUGHTER and here she is. She's tiny and wonderful and has a huge birthmark on her right leg. I have two names in mind — Wanda and Deborah — but I want Billy to have a part in her birth so I let him choose. He picks Deborah and I'm glad. I think a name beginning with a hard consonant will give her character strength.

I look forward to the same relaxed, contented time I had with Billy when he was a baby. It's not going to happen. While I'm in the hospital, Bill rents an old two-storey row house. Now Billy has to go to a different school, three blocks away. We quickly go through my savings with nothing to show for it and with Bill doing only casual labour we're always low on money.

We buy a washing machine and discover, after we've wrestled it into our basement, that it doesn't work. If Bill is gone with the car, I have to carry Debbie and a bag of laundry a long ways every couple of days, and in winter this isn't easy. I have to time it around having to walk Billy to school and back, in the mornings, lunchtimes, and after school.

What bothers me the most is that we don't even have a crib for Debbie. After five years of working and saving I should have been financially prepared for Debbie's new life. Instead, I'm worse off than when Billy was born because now I have two children to look after. I sink into a deep depression.

In December Bill leaves us. Already fragile, I sink even lower. I hate Bill for leaving. I HATE him! And what kind of mother am I, choosing a father like that? He doesn't deserve to be a father. I don't deserve to be a mother. I'm tired and I'm sick. For my children's sake, I should give them up. Poor Billy — after school one day, I notice him watching me, and I see in his eyes that he is wondering why I'm always so sad. I realize I'm making him sad too. I've let him down. And I can't stand it! That night in bed, I cry as quietly as I can. I don't want to give him and Debbie up, especially not to CAS, but what choice do I have?

The next morning, my eyes are swollen, I feel listless and my heart aches. After taking Billy to school, I cry the whole morning. What am I going to do? Give them up and give them a chance? Keeping them would be so selfish. I have nothing useful to give. If I keep them, I'll just drag them down with me.

After lunch I bundle Debbie up and we walk Billy to school. Before returning home, I walk to the closest payphone and call Children's Aid. Back at home, before I even have Debbie out of her winter bunting bag, I begin crying again — and wonder if I'll ever stop.

Although I have no thought of committing suicide, I must have told CAS about my sister's suicide to stress how desperately I need help. They send a social worker — a male social worker. First he tells me that suicide runs in families. Then he makes a pass at me.

I call CAS again. This time they send a homemaker. She is from the Caribbean and after a few days, she tells me that there are bad spirits in the house and she can't come back anymore. Well, they aren't my bad spirits because I also had that feeling, right from the day we moved in, and I don't even believe in such things. Then again, maybe it is me — my bleak depression.

After she leaves, I have a moment of clarity, like a bit of sun shining through an opening in heavy thunderclouds. I realize I am so grateful that CAS didn't take my children, as I thought they would. I have an opportunity to figure out what to do, without the suffocating self-pity. The first thing is to go to the welfare office. I've heard they can make you wait all day, so I call Tanya to see if she will baby-sit Debbie, while Billy and I go. I get some money for food and I'm told to come back for rent money. Tanya invites us to stay for supper. When I tell her how I've been feeling, she offers to take Billy and Debbie until I get back on my feet. She's tells me that my depression is the baby blues, and that it won't last. What a lifesaver she is!

While my children stay at her place, I rent a room in a downtown building. Finally, my unemployment cheques start to arrive, and I've never had so much money in my life. That sun is shining a little bit stronger. Now if I can get a job lined up, I can find us a place to stay.

It's also time to heal myself and deal with my guilt over considering letting CAS take my children. The main library is within easy walking distance and I go there to find books about psychology and psychiatry. I don't think I have a psychiatric disorder. I just need to shake my feeling of being weak and helpless. As I read, I discern that the way therapy works is not for the doctor to tell you what's wrong with you; but that by answering the doctor's questions, you eventually understand what your problem is. By understanding the problem, you can then solve it. Usually, you are responsible for getting yourself into that place of despair; therefore, you should own up to it, and be responsible for getting yourself out. You own your problem and you own the solution. You empower yourself. That's my conclusion, at least for now.

Well, my problem is Bill. No, my problem is my attachment to Bill. With almost everyone, even Mom and Dad, I figure that if they don't want to be with me, then I don't want to be with them. Problem solved. Vivian and, later, Bill could turn me to mush. When they were there I would give just about anything to remain with them. If Vivian were still alive, she and Bill would be the only two people who could leave me, reject me, betray me, whatever, but I would always forgive them.

Why? I have only a partial answer in Bill's case. He's the father of my children. And while Mr. Chevalier was a good foster father to me, I don't want a foster father for my children. I want their real father to be a real father. So much for self-empowerment. Obviously, I'm not asking myself the right questions yet, but the exercise is important, as I'm beginning to feel much better. And it will help me deal with what is yet to come.

MY SISTER- AND BROTHER-in-law, Anita and Ryan, are now living in an area of Winnipeg called Transcona. I contact them at the right time because they tell me about a house for rent. They know the landlord and the house, and they'll vouch for me. I tell them I will rent it. January 24th, 1973, is a Wednesday and in the evening I go to Transcona to bring Anita and Ryan the rent to pass on to the landlord. I leave their place at about 9:00 p.m. At night, it can be about a two-hour bus trip home.

At around 10:30, I'm a block from home, walking by a parking lot when a car turns into it. As I wait for a light to change, two men from that car come on either side of me and ask if I want to go to a party. I don't answer. They grab hold of my arms and pull me back toward their car. Across the street is a bus, and I am sure the bus driver can see that I'm struggling to free myself and will help. He doesn't.

The men throw me into the back seat of the car. I land on my back. I kick at the windows but can't break them. Besides if I did, that would just increase their anger, and it wouldn't allow me to escape. The men jump in the front seats, and the driver snarls that I had better quit kicking or they'll beat me up. I sit up and try to keep track of where they're driving. Since they haven't bothered to disguise themselves, I'm sure they will kill me. There's a metal toolbox on the backseat floor and I press my fingers to all the sides to leave my fingerprints. I also watch for a police car because if I see one, I'll do something to the driver to make the police stop the car. But too soon we're out of the city on dark roads.

The car stops and I try to prepare myself mentally for what is to come. I have to remain alert for a chance to get out. I don't plead because that will not help; it will just give them more power. The driver seems like a lunatic and I sense he intimidates his accomplice. At the same time, I can't believe I'm in this situation and I am terrified. I keep thinking: I don't want to die; I don't want to die. This isn't my time to die. Oh God, not this way.

The driver gets in the back. Throughout the rape, he calls me squaw, bitch, cunt, and other vile names. He tells me I want it. He tells me I like it. He tells me to say those things. I don't. He slaps me hard across my face when I try to stop him from undressing me. He forces me onto my stomach. I hear him pulling at his jeans. Then he's inside me. I bear the brunt of his penetration passively. When he's done, he turns me on my back and he's inside me again. I watch his crazy lunatic face, wondering how I can possibly escape.

The passenger asks the driver for a turn and, after they exchange places, he asks the driver if he should go down on me. The driver almost gives him instructions. This must be his first rape. That means he's the weak link, the one who might protect me from being killed. He finishes quickly and I'm disheartened when they change places again because I'm so terrified of the driver.

I look at his hands for the knife I imagine he has. He doesn't have a knife but he has something else in mind. He pulls down his jeans and tells me to suck. He warns me that if I bite, I'll regret it. Silently, I refuse. He pulls my head to his penis and forces it into my mouth. I choke and try to pull back, but he has me in a tight grip. He moves my head back and forth. I gag. Then I hear him say to his accomplice, "I wonder how much her tits weigh."

The tone he uses is to imply to me that they have weighed women's breasts before. To do that, they would have had to cut them off, wouldn't they? That image sends my terror, already at its peak, I thought, sky-rocketing. To die is bad enough. To be tortured to death is worse.

Then he says, "I feel like a piss," and with that he pisses into my mouth. The passenger yells at him not to get the car dirty. I start to retch, making the passenger even more agitated. He panics, yells for the driver to get me out of the car. Hearing the panic in his voice, I keep making retching sounds, even though the need to vomit has passed. The driver hauls me out and throws my clothes out after me. I keep retching so they don't change their minds. The driver jumps in the front and the car speeds away.

I try to see the license plate but can't. Without my glasses I can't see much of anything from just the car's rear lights. I am so relieved to be out of that car. I was so sure that they were going to kill me, but here I am. Alive!

CHAPTER 13

I DRESS, FIND MY GLASSES, and look around. There are no houses nearby, but in the far distance, in the direction the car went, I can see what must be a road light. I walk as fast as I can, staying in the tire tracks so I don't leave footprints in the snow. I have to get away from where they threw me out because that's where they'll begin looking for me if they come back. If I see headlights coming, I'll hide in the field.

The light turns out to be a farmyard light, and as I walk into the driveway, thunderous barking erupts from a huge German shepherd as it approaches me. I'm relieved to see it because right now I need a connection to the animal world. A porch light goes on as I knock on the door.

A man opens it and looks at me cautiously. I blurt out that I've been raped and could he please call the police. His wife comes up behind him and they invite me in. She makes coffee while I use their washroom to rinse out my mouth. When I return, I shiver so uncontrollably that the woman wraps me in a blanket. Their kindness coming after the viciousness of the rapists makes me cry.

RCMP officers arrive and take me back to where I'd been thrown out of the car. They seem angry with the rapists and in a way their anger helps a bit. I thought they wouldn't believe me or would figure I'd asked for it — the usual stereotype: Native women will go off with any man who offers them booze. Surrounded by four white people, I'm very conscious of this, especially as none of them knows whether I had been drinking or not.

From there, the police take me to the hospital, where a nurse swabs me for evidence, then back to my place to change, because I have to give the police the clothing I'd been wearing, including my winter coat. Then they take me to their detachment, where I have to recount every detail of the rape. As I tell it, I tremble uncontrollably again, even though I'm no longer cold — well, not on the outside. Finally, they drive me home.

It's after four in the morning. Other tenants share the bathroom, but I need to get clean. I lock the door and stack things in front of it so that anyone trying to come in will make noise. While the water runs hot, I wash out my mouth and brush my teeth. I *should have bitten off his penis. No, it was more important to stay alive.* In the bathtub, I scrub myself with the facecloth and lots of soap, but still don't feel clean. If I'd had a brush I would have scrubbed myself raw. I am so angry with those two men. I wish over and over that I could have castrated them, but the thought doesn't help. I will have to take many more long hot baths to get rid of the feel of them on me and in me, and to get rid of their smell. It will become a ritual.

In the following days the thought that comforts me is that I'm alive. I also realize that I had not once thought of my children while I was in that car. They had not belonged in the same place of such evil. I believed I had been in a struggle for my life and I had to concentrate on all that was happening so I could live. After my initial attempt to kick out the windows, I think becoming passive is what got me out alive. I survived the rape and now I have to survive the aftermath.

The negativity of having the baby blues now becomes an advantage because in trying to heal myself from the depression, I'd read all those books. The one idea that sticks with me is that if you own the problem, you must also own the solution. And the first part of my solution is to find the rapists' car, find them, and have them arrested. And I just happen to know a gutsy person who can help me.

I call on my old friend, Bobbie, from the days of the Hungry Eye, and it's as if we had never lost touch. She is now married to a soldier stationed in Germany, and is joining him soon. She still has her gentle collie, and now has a big new Jeep. We spend many nights driving around downtown, looking for the car; but we don't find it. Since she's leaving for Germany, our search comes to an end. So much for that part of the solution.

In preparation for my rape trial — if it ever happens — I attend one. Then I get the idea that since the driver seemed to be singling out Native girls, I might find others who had been raped by him. I learn about a Native justice organization in the North End, that provides information and translators for people going to court, and I make an appointment with a court worker, Dorothy Betz.

As I walk to her office, I'm trying to figure out what to say. Will she be hard or easy to talk to? Will she assume that I had been drinking? In the office hall, a woman and a small elderly woman pass by and, deep in my own thoughts, I pay them no attention. But again, like when I saw my Dad, a familiar weird sensation comes over me. I stop and turn.

"Mom?"

The small elderly woman turns and, sure enough, it's Mom! The last time I saw her had been about ten years ago, in December 1963. She waits while I speak with the court worker, who is amazed: she has appointments first with Clara Mosionier and then with Beatrice Culleton and they turn out to be mother and daughter! If I weren't there for my reason, I'd probably share in her amazement. Awkwardly I interrupt with my explanation of why I made the appointment. She isn't aware of other rape victims, but she says she will put the word out and get them to contact the officer in charge of my case. Nothing will come of it.

Mom and I go for coffee. She seems so happy to see me that I'm not going to take away her happiness by telling her I was raped. My mind is on the rape and my disappointment in not finding other Native rape victims and I'm now trying to figure out what else I can do. I try to pay attention to what Mom's saying. She senses that I'm distracted. We're like strangers. I think we've always been strangers. She looks so much older than I remember. I want to ask if she went back to drinking, but of course, I don't. I tell her about Billy and Debbie, and that conversation soon dies out. She gives me her address and we part.

The next thing I do is to join a rape crisis group, in hopes of finding other Native victims. I'm the only Native woman in the group and I quit after a couple of meetings. I do learn, however, that rape is not a sexual act. It's physical assault by which a rapist 'dis-empowers' his victim. I also learn that rapists are like predators in that they pick out women who put out signals that they're potential victims. For us, just by being Native, we are potential victims. Still, such a blanket statement rankles me because it's saying that all rape victims have had a hand in their being victimized.

Later it occurs to me: if Native victims had been drinking, and maybe even if they hadn't, would they go to the police? No. Would they go to some organization for help? No. So I won't look any more. I will have to be the only witness against those two rapists and hope people in court will take my word.

BECAUSE THE HOUSE I rented is vacant, the landlord lets us move in before the end of February. I haven't found a job, so I have time to be with Debbie and Billy. I enroll Billy in kindergarten and go looking for used furniture. The first thing I buy is a crib for Debbie. Then I find a washing machine, making sure it works before I buy it. The next thing I get is a telephone. Anita and Ryan are a big help, baby-sitting and getting my furniture moved in.

Once in a while the police officers pick me up and take me to look at mug shots and, once, a Vega car. Because it was dark out, I wasn't sure of the colour of the car. I certainly don't want to accuse the wrong men. I'm able to make a sketch of the passenger, but perhaps because he terrified me, something blocks me from being able to sketch the driver. Out of hundreds of mug shots I look at, not one jumps out at me.

One day, I'm walking along Regent Avenue West, the main street in Transcona. A man walks toward me. He's white, a businessman, in a dark suit and overcoat. There is nothing menacing about him and he doesn't even look at me. Yet I feel such a sudden terror that I have to turn and watch, make sure he's not going to grab me. He gives me no reason for this feeling, but I recognize it as an after-effect of the rape. Over the next few months I will get this feeling of terror again and again when I encounter men. I hate it that I can't control these sudden feelings. I become anxious when I have to go out, even to the job I find. I'm soon fired for making a mistake.

I HAVE BEEN GOING to a women's clinic for post-natal check-ups. On this one occasion the staff seems really sympathetic. The head nurse takes me into her office and tells me they have the results of my last test. I have cancer of the uterus and should put my house in order. From the sound of it, I have only a few weeks to live.

Amazingly, I don't feel sorry for myself or even scared of dying. It's business first: I wonder if I should ask Anita and Ryan if they would look after my children. I have no one else. But they have two kids and only a small two-bedroom house. That night I look in on my baby daughter and my five-year old son. They are sleeping so peacefully, with no idea that I'm going to cause them one final upheaval. That's when I decide that I am not going to die. I didn't survive the rape to die now. I am going to live!

CHAPTER 14

I N THE FOLLOWING DAYS AND WEEKS, I wait for the pain to hit. Cancer
is painful. But the pain never comes. What does come is a letter of
apology from the hospital: they had inadvertently mislabelled someone
else's test. I'm feeling like a steeplechaser who has to jump hurdle after
hurdle. I stumbled badly at the first one — the baby blues, and was hurt
at the second — the rape; but I think I'm getting the hang of it now.

By April 1973 I get a part-time job in a small, downtown law firm.
The money is enough to pay for everything I need and I'll be home for
Billy before and after school. Billy tells me that the mother of a friend in
his class lives just down the back lane and she could baby-sit Debbie. He
takes me to meet her. Like me, she's Native.

I'M NOT SURPRISED when Bill comes back. Because of the rape, I don't
want him around. I do want him around. It's intimacy I don't want even
though I know now that rape has nothing to do with making love. I tell
him about the rape in a blurting-it-out kind of way. Instead of giving
me sympathy or even feeling sorry for me, he runs up some bills for
a motorcycle and other things he needs. Not knowing what I'm in for,
I co-sign his loan from a finance company. Then Bill rides off on the
motorcycle, leaving me to pay his debts, and wishing I'd kept my mouth
shut about the rape. In late spring I get an unexpected income-tax

refund so I'm able to pay the bills off. For the first time since I've known Bill, I'm convinced I will never see him again. If I do I'll give him a piece of my mind and send him on his way. That's it! I've had enough and I'll never let him smooth-talk his way back into my life again.

ONE AFTERNOON I ASK Billy and his friends to get me a quart of milk at the corner store. I give him the last of my money and off they go. When Billy hands me the container, I see that they must have all been sipping from it. I won't be able to pour milk from that dirty spout into my coffee, but I can't help laughing.

ONE DAY I GO to the lunch counter at a department store near the office. I take a stool and wait my turn. The service seems slow until I notice people around me coming and going and being served almost immediately. I then realize the waitress is ignoring me. I'm too shy to speak up, but the longer I wait, the more stubborn I get. I refuse to leave. She refuses to make eye contact. Peripherally, I see that other customers have noticed and a few squirm uncomfortably. That's when my stubbornness wavers and a lump comes to my throat. Now I couldn't speak even if I wanted to. Still, I stay until I have no choice but to go back to work.

Another day before most of the office staff has to testify in a court case, our boss, Mr. Marek, takes us to lunch. Everyone orders drinks, me included. He says to me, "Do you think that's wise? You have to testify." Everyone freezes and someone gives an audible groan. So even my boss thinks that no Native person can handle liquor. Since he's paying, I leave my drink untouched.

MY BABY-SITTER GOES back to work full time and the new one lives a very long walk away and nowhere near a bus route. So I carry Debbie and her diaper bag all the way there and then walk almost as far again to catch a bus. The good news is her husband is a karate instructor.

I have desperately wanted to get into martial arts ever since I was terrified by the innocent businessman passing me on the sidewalk, but I'm reluctant to walk into a strange place and ask how much it would cost. If it were out of my price range, the possibility of taking a course would disappear. Because I like the idea of having a choice, I've procrastinated. Now the baby-sitter encourages me to take classes. I finally explain the reason for my reluctance, so the instructor offers me a really cheap rate in exchange for keeping the books for the karate club. That works for me and I enroll.

Gradually, I learn the first Kata, the simplest series of blocks, punches, and kicks, well enough to practise at home. Occasionally far more advanced students spar with the beginners and one time I get kicked in the thigh. Amazingly it doesn't hurt but immediately comes up in a huge bruise. Another time a man with a black belt accidentally punches me in the midriff. He is so alarmed I wonder if I'm supposed to drop dead. I laugh it off and we continue. I was so afraid of being beaten up when I was being raped, it would have been good to have known that getting punched and kicked doesn't hurt as much as I thought it would, even though I wouldn't have acted differently.

As we get closer to being tested, we have to do our Katas alone. The black belts study our every move and offer opinions or corrections. My impulse is to quit because I'll be too shy to do it. I don't quit though and when my turn does come, I concentrate on doing the best I can and do reasonably well. As I progress, I lose my fear of the street and gain tranquility. I'm not healed — that may take years — but I'm on my way. I have no idea if I could defend myself against two men, but now I would give it my all. When I get to the second level, I enroll Billy. Learning martial arts improves discipline and focus and I think he would enjoy it as much as I do.

After one class, a group stays for a board meeting. We're all sitting on the floor in a circle when someone notices a big black spider in the center. We all move back, even the brown and black belts. Finally one of the members lets it crawl onto his paper and he shakes it out the window. Imagine that — all these big tough guys share my apprehension about spiders. And, rather than kill it, they put it outside. I like that.

I'VE BEEN ABLE TO save some money and decide to buy a car. I don't want to go to finance companies because of their high interest rates, so I ask my boss to recommend me to the credit union. When the loan is approved, I buy a used Dodge Monaco. Having a car gives me greater freedom. Now I can take the kids on outings I wouldn't have been able to before.

Mr. Marek can have extreme highs and lows. At times he is excitable or very ill-tempered and at other times, he is genial and funny. He's been through many secretaries and one of the latest is Moira, who is from England. When a transit strike hits, I drive her to and from work. Another woman from her apartment building asks to join us. When the strike is over and she no longer needs a ride, she tells Moira she shouldn't be friends with me because I'm Native.

Over lunch in the office, Moira asks me about Indian people. As I tell her what I know, Patty, one of the other secretaries, is kicking her under the table and looking uncomfortable. Later, when Moira asks her why, Patty says, "Well, you were asking Beatrice about Native people and she's Native." Moira tells her that's why she asked. When Moira tells me Patty's reply — "You don't talk about Native people in front of them" — we laugh at Patty's twisted logic. In reality, though, I laugh to cover the hurt I feel from Patty's attitude and the embarrassment of being part of a group that is always on the receiving end of racist attitudes.

When Debbie turns three I'm able to enroll her in a downtown, subsidized daycare centre with nearby parking. One winter morning the roads are pure ice. My Dodge had been rear ended a few days earlier, so I'm in a loaner car from the repair shop. On Regent Avenue, I'm in the slow lane when a vehicle in front suddenly slows to make a right-hand turn. I brake and try to move to the left lane. Bad move. The little Gremlin glides to the other side of Regent, jumps the curb, narrowly missing a streetlight pole, continues across the ditch and ends up almost underneath a large billboard, advertising a car, that reads, "Take a Closer Look."

Debbie is still in her place in the back seat, looking puzzled, as if she realizes this isn't our usual route. The back window is busted out but I don't see any other damage. A police car is in the oncoming traffic that we have fortunately missed crashing into, and the officers come to help. They have us sit in their car and that's when Debbie starts bawling. After they write a report, they drive us all the way downtown to Debbie's daycare.

ONE OF THE KARATE students is also a single parent and we've become good friends. He tells me that when I do my taxes, I can claim one of my children as "equivalent-to-married." Oh, that sounds so incestuous to me that I don't quite believe it. Sure enough the line is on the form, so I fill it in. Then I wait for the taxman to come knocking at my door. In the meantime, I use the refund to pay off my car loan.

HAVING VISITED MOM A few times, I ask her if she would like to come live with us and baby-sit Debbie, and she agrees. She has a great sense of humour and, as she tells me about Debbie's day, we laugh a lot. We never talk about the past, except for good memories, funny things. I have to work at not asking questions that will raise painful memories, as she never goes to the dark places. While she can find humour in what must have been a hard life, sometimes I feel as if we are walking on eggshells and our laughter seems forced.

It all works out until the day I come home from work and see that she has been drinking. Somehow she got herself some beer. Later when the kids are sleeping, she nurses another beer. I try to talk with her but she just babbles nonsense and raises her voice. I've never seen her like this. I'm shocked. Does she always get this way when she drinks? The next morning she seems fine, but when I return from work and find that she's been drinking again, I'm gripped by anger that goes all the way back to my childhood and I tell her she has to leave. I settle her in with some downtown friends and drive away, feeling guilty. But I can't have her drinking in front of my kids.

MY LANDLORD DECIDES TO sell our house and I decide to buy it. After the bank turns me down, Mr. Marek vouches for me once again with the credit union and I get my mortgage. At last we have our own home. The house may be old, with a trap door to an unfinished basement and an old add-on shed, but it's ours. With its two small bedrooms, it's nothing like the dream houses I designed when I was young, but it's ours, and I love it. Well actually, it's not really ours until I pay off the mortgage, but this is so much better than paying rent. Nobody will ever make us move again. And if I said that before, this time, I really mean it.

ABOUT SEVEN YEARS back, after Larry left, Kathy moved from Auntie Ada's and for a long time I didn't know where she was. She had met a sales representative for a printing company and had landed a steady job in the shipping department of a large appliance company in Ajax, Ontario. Now she comes to Winnipeg for a two-week visit. On Friday when I get home from work, she wants to visit the bars she used to go to. We go to pick up Mom and her two sisters, who are visiting from out of town. Since others also want to come with us, I park the car and we all walk toward Main Street. Inside the beverage room, I kind of feel trapped. I don't like the bar scene and can't understand what the attraction is, so I just sip on my Coke as my resentment grows.

A young white man who had been going around to other tables asks if he can join us. He introduces himself as a university student and says he is doing a thesis or something on Main Street bars. My translation: he's writing up his preconceptions about drunken Main Street Natives. I tell Mom not to talk to him.

Apparently Mom gets very sociable when she first starts drinking and invites him to sit next to her. He asks Mom why she likes coming here — the very question I've been pondering, except that he's white and I'm not, so from him it sounds patronizing. Before Mom can answer, I ask him if he always comes down to these bars to feel superior to the people here. He tries to explain his good intentions, but I cut him off with a barrage of sarcastic questions and accusations. I'm so rude he leaves the bar. I lick my chops. Good, one down. Bring on the next one.

I don't even have the excuse of drinking for my rudeness. What I do have is a flash of the rage I used to get when I was a kid. I don't know if that man brought it on, or if he just got in the way of my resentment at being in the bar. Until tonight I've only seen the effects of Main Street beverage rooms from the outside. Now here I am, inside, and it's the last place I want to be.

Kathy's visit is way too short, especially since we wasted time in bars, even though she never got drunk and neither did anyone else, including Mom. During her stay Kathy shows me an old newspaper photograph of a little girl. It's her when she was 11 and had won a jigging contest. She tells me that Dad was a fiddle player and won many contests. I had never heard about any of that — not at family visits or even from Mom, when she was living with me. I've always loved music and now I think I must get that from Dad. Too bad we don't know where he is because it would have been great for Kathy and Dad to see each other.

Billy and I are sitting on the couch, watching TV. He runs his hand along my forearm and asks, "How come you're this colour?" I look down at his white hand on my brown arm and reply, "I have more Indian blood in me than you do. God made me this colour." From his tone, I wonder if his two Native friends, who are as dark as I am, were being called names and it bothered Billy. Maybe that made him suddenly aware of my colouring. I don't know if my answer is right, or enough, but I don't have any instinct on what more to say. Besides I don't want to make a big deal out of this because I don't want him focused on skin colour. I want him to accept people of any race, as they are. At this time I think that being colour-blind is a good thing.

At the end of Billy's grade-2 year, the principal wants to meet with me. They will be dividing the classes: one for the smarter kids who can work well in an open setting, and a smaller one for the slow learners. Billy and his Native friend will be with the slow learners. His white friend is going into the smart class. At parent-teacher meetings I'd been told that Billy was doing well. He was even advanced in his language skills. From the way the principal talks and looks at me, I feel the real problem is racism.

My first reaction is to get out of that office as fast as I can. A lump has come to my throat and I can't speak. I also don't want the principal to see my tears. When I get home, I cry because I've just discovered how helpless I am to protect my children against racism. I've taken the ugly looks, the biting remarks, the bullying, the smugness, the subtle innuendoes and more. True, I've had no choice. Even though my children are fair-skinned, they'll experience the same things I have. And I don't know how to keep them from feeling that pain.

My second reaction to the principal's racism is to transfer Billy to a Catholic school the following September. What I had not considered was that he would have to learn catechism so he would come to realize I commit mortal sins by not taking him to church on Sundays. When I was first on my own, after Children's Aid, I attended Sunday mass, but by the time I had met Bill, I had stopped going. The superstitions remained with me long enough to have Billy baptized. By the time Debbie was born I did not believe in the church at all, having gotten rid of the superstitions, so I didn't have her baptized. Unfortunately, I don't have an alternate belief system to teach my children. When they get older, I want them to be open to all religions.

In the shorter term I have to rethink my reactive decision to put Billy in the Catholic school. Yes they have racism in the public school; but in the Catholic school, they teach a God-given justification for it. And that's harder to fight. How do I explain to Billy what I perceive to be the church's failings without turning him against the Catholic religion? Some of their teachings are really good. I do want him to be kind and thoughtful to others, no matter what they do to him. Well, I can teach him that by example. I decide that in the new school year I will put him back in public school. I caution myself about being so reactive because, once again, I brought emotional confusion into Billy's childhood years.

I QUIT TAKING KARATE classes because the *sensei* is now insisting that we all have to yell our *kiais* when we do the Katas. I cannot yell; therefore I cannot advance. Besides karate has done for me what I wanted it to do. Mentally, emotionally, and physically, I am much stronger than when I started. The unexpected racism of Billy's principal set me back. On the good side for me at least, it forced me to think about parenting as a Native person, which I wouldn't have otherwise considered.

BILL RETURNS AND visits us, and Billy is so happy and excited that it jars me. In the past I sometimes felt I was so focused on the pain that Bill caused me that I never considered what Billy was going through. I finally understand that, while I still love Bill, he will never change. Now there is only one thing I want from him and that is a divorce. It becomes final in July 1974.

I expected that Bill would go back to Toronto but he doesn't. Every time he visits, Billy's eyes light up and he seems happier, somehow more whole. It isn't that he's a sad child when he's with me — both he and Debbie are such a pleasure I know I must be doing something right. But I also know that, for Billy especially, life could be better. Haunted by the sadness in his eyes when I was so depressed, I much prefer the joyful look that his father brings to them.

It seemed that back in the spring of 1969, when we were first married, Bill was so secure that I would never leave him that he felt free to run off with another woman that very same year. If we did get back together again, well, now that we're divorced, he would think twice about walking out the door. If he did, we both know that would be the end of us. So in October, I let Bill move back in.

CHAPTER 15

ONE OF BILL'S COUSINS, FRED, CONVINCES Bill to get into long-distance trucking in December. The money is the best Bill's ever made. Soon he decides our two-bedroom house is too small — it is — so we sell it to put a down payment on a newer, bigger three-bedroom bilevel.

FOR THE PAST FEW YEARS the RCMP had maintained contact with me, but as time passed, the contact became less and less. However, because I thought the rapists might be caught and I'd get my day in court, I had kept everything that happened on that January night, alive — alive, but in the back of my mind as I didn't want to let it control my everyday life with my family and work. In February 1976, an officer calls to tell me there's nothing new to report and it doesn't look promising. By now I almost tell him that I don't want to go to court anymore. I want to put that night out of my mind for good. I don't want to think about it anymore. But I know I have to see this through to the end. Those rapists were probably terrorizing other Native women. After I hang up, I'm resentful of all those Native women who are raped and don't report it, especially those who may have encountered the men who raped me. I wonder to myself why I should care about other Native women. If they're not reporting rapes, then they're helping their rapists go on victimizing, helping them to remain free. However, my resentment doesn't last because I do understand their side of it.

BECAUSE HE KNOWS I love horses, Bill buys me an Appaloosa named Judy. I'm thrilled, but Judy does not like her new home and gets out. Bill repairs the fence but she gets out again. Bill decides we should move to a bigger house with 75 acres, just north of Stony Mountain. By now I have a live-in baby-sitter and she agrees to move with us.

I get Billy into the 4H club and we learn much more about horses and riding. In the evenings I saddle Judy and Sam, a pony Bill got for Billy, and we ride along the local dirt roads. One time I have Judy at a full gallop and I feel that she is running like the wind. Then out of the corner of my eye, I notice Sam: it looks like he is only trotting as they pass us. I laugh so hard that I almost fall off.

That summer is great. Four-year-old Debbie decides to learn how to ride her bike. At first I help a bit and then go off to do some yard work; but later I stop to watch. She won't give up: she almost gets it, loses her balance, picks herself up, and begins again. Over and over she does this, for days, until she's proudly riding smoothly. I love her determination; that's what I lacked when I had learned to ride a bike. Or maybe I was just plain lazy: if at first you don't succeed, why bother?

AT THE BEGINNING of October I get a letter from the RCMP. Over a year and a half has passed since I last talked to an officer. Now they're terminating the investigation and they'll be mailing my clothing back. When I finish reading the letter, I think I've been more fortunate than most rape victims, because I had read those books after my depression, and I had taken karate. Both helped me deal with the memories of the rape. What this letter means for me now is that I can let those memories fade away. Well, aren't those rapists lucky my voice will not be heard? What I will learn in the future is that memories of such trauma don't really fade away. Memories of the rape will always be with me but they will not control my life.

SUMMER DAYS ARE long gone, autumn slips by, and winter sets in. I knew that this was how the seasons worked when we moved to Stony Mountain but the lure of having our own horses was greater than the thought of having to make the long winter drives to and from work. I haven't forgotten the accident I had because of ice. I don't know how Bill deals with his stress of highway driving. At times I wish I could be a stay-at-home mother.

I GET A CONSTANT ringing in my ears. When I can't stand it anymore, I go to a hearing specialist. The tests show a hearing loss in my right ear from nerve damage. The specialist tells me a hearing aid will only increase the volume of the garble.

IN THE SPRING WE have to put the house up for sale: the large mortgage and the horses have us in over our heads. Bill finds a really cheap farm on a quarter section in Vita, about 85 miles south of Winnipeg. The only thing new on it is a large barn and it'll be good for the horses. I quit my job and we move at the end of the school year.

Bill buys his own rig and he now does long-distance hauling as an owner-operator. I do the bookkeeping. At last I have my own desk and office equipment. I have my car and Bill gets a used pick-up truck to drive to his rig in Winnipeg. The down side is that in Stony Mountain we had a big modern house; this house uses wood for heating, is much smaller, and is a two-storey.

Fred lives just outside Portage la Prairie and when he's home from highway driving, he gives me riding lessons. The horse I ride is a quarter-horse stallion named Pistol. On my birthday Fred arrives with a horse trailer. Bill has bought Pistol for me as a birthday present. He also gets a female Maltese puppy and finally I get to name an animal and come up with Lady. Later we get a black quarter-horse foal named Paco, and a pregnant Holstein cow named Rosie.

I REFLECT ON OUR past as I'm beginning to feel that all the waiting I did for Bill to accept his responsibilities was worth it. I won't ever marry him again because while I think he'll never leave me again, he could. We talk at a deeper level than we ever did in our first seven years and so I understand him much more than I understood him in the early years. What Bill had given me right in the beginning was a sense of home. My childhood yearning to go back home to my own family had been fulfilled when I met him. He had told me then and still tells me that I am special to him. As a teenager, I felt I had adapted to not being loved or ever being the favourite in anybody else's life. I think he is the first person in my life who ever loved me, in a way that I wanted to be loved. And I had been so grateful for that. Somebody loved me! In return I had given him my love tenfold. Now I'm at peace, in a place of contentment, and I realize it's not because of him. It's because of me!

THE FARMHOUSE WAS BUILT well but isn't insulated and has only a woodburning furnace. In the fall we gather wood and I insist on only deadwood. When we've gathered more than four cords cut to furnace lengths, Bill figures that should do us. The deadwood burns very fast so I have to get up a few times during winter nights to feed the furnace. Still, the pipes freeze and burst. After they're fixed, we spend hours trying to prime the water pump from the well.

The shorter pieces of wood soon run out and I have to learn how to use the chain saw to cut the larger pieces for splitting. Mornings and evenings Billy has to feed all the animals. After the kids go to school, I clean out the barn. Towards the end of winter we run low on wood, so on sunny days, I don't burn any while the kids are at school. Bill buys a woodstove for the main floor, and when he's away, we sleep in the living room where it's warmer. That is the longest, coldest winter we have experienced, and finally it is springtime.

AROUND NOON ONE day Rosie is trying to give birth but is having difficulties. Bill sends me over to a neighbour's farm for help. When I get there I see they are having lunch. I explain the situation and politely ask if the farmer would come over when he's finished his meal. He jumps up, grabs a calving chain off the wall, and hurries with me to our place. He attaches the chain to the hooves of the calf and pulls. Finally a big chocolate brown calf is lying at Rosie's feet and is soon up and nursing.

All is well. Now the farmer has time to laugh at me because I had expected him to finish his lunch before helping. Whenever we meet after that, he reminds me and laughs some more.

WHEN IT'S TIME TO cut the alfalfa and timothy, Bill buys a tractor and all the equipment we'll need to harvest and bale the crops. Because he's away on the road, I'm the one who ends up spending days driving the tractor up and down the fields, mowing and later, raking. When he's home, he changes the equipment on the tractor, repairs machinery, and does all the heavy work that I can't do.

When we aren't working, we exchange visits, often with a neighbour, Linda, who lives three miles away. She has two girls and two boys. Tanya and her family moved from the city back to their cabin in Piney and are about a half hour away. Our farmer neighbour has three boys who are friends with Billy, and Anita's boys come for a couple of weeks during the summer. So my children have lots of friends and love living in Vita.

Throughout the summer and fall we build up cords of firewood. Now I let Bill cut fresh wood. We have insulated the water pipes, but the basement still needs to be kept warm enough so that no water freezes. If it does, I have to wait until Bill comes off the road to drain the system, fix the pipes, and prime the pump. I still cut and split wood throughout the winter, but I have a little more time to help with feeding the animals.

TWO STRAY DOGS TAKE up residence with us. Billy names them Dusty and Saber. Then a third dog shows up; Debbie names him Tramp and he becomes her favourite outside dog. Only Lady is an inside dog. One morning Debbie phones me from school, crying. She says that the school bus ran over Tramp and the driver wouldn't stop. I go outside, hoping that she was mistaken. But Tramp is lying on the road, dead. I carry him back into our yard and, when Bill gets home, we bury him in the woods.

IN MARCH 1980, I get a letter from Mrs. Chevalier. Ever since I moved back to Winnipeg I have kept in touch with her. She writes that Mary

Flatfoot died of liver disease, on February 18th, in Vancouver. The nuns are taking care of her daughter, Lisa.

Her letter takes me back to when Mary, Marla, and I were still living at the Chevaliers'. Mr. Chevalier and the three of us had been sitting at the table after supper, talking about babies. Mary piped up that she wanted three. Mr. Chevalier had looked at her across the table and, because of her polio, said, "You'll never be able to have children." Mary looked as if he had just slapped her across the face. Marla and I didn't say anything, but I wondered how Mr. Chevalier, usually a kind man, could have been so thoughtless.

Well, Mary had proved him wrong.

I had never forgotten — or forgiven — Mr. Chevalier's rude remark to Mary. Yet on the whole, he had been a fantastic foster father. I felt that if he had been Mary's real father, his remark might have sounded different to me and been forgivable. That may not be logical, but it was one of the reasons why I had stuck it out with Bill.

WE HAVE A SMALL grain shack inside the cow pasture, where we keep the oats and bags of feed. One day I find Rosie and her calf with their heads stuck through the small opening in the side of the shack, where the cover had not been put on properly. Because of their horns, they can't get out. I figure the only way to get them out is to cut their horns off. So I look through my books to find out how to dehorn cattle, but there's no such information. Then it comes to me: if I can't cut their horns off, I can cut the hole bigger — as long as they don't get panicked by the sound of a buzzing jigsaw next to their ears.

I get the jigsaw and begin. Rosie and her calf remain calm, almost as if they know I'm helping them. Finally the hole is large enough for them to get free. To have even considered cutting off their horns, how stupid was I?

WE HAVE BOUGHT A new stove and fridge, my first brand new appliances ever. I bake pies and make all sorts of recipes from *The Joy of Cooking*. When the freezer is full, I recover, remembering how much I hate being in the kitchen. But I do invite the Chevaliers for supper. Mrs. Chevalier tells me that Lily, who had a civil marriage like Bill and me, got her marriage blessed. Mrs. Chevalier says I should get my marriage blessed. That's when I tell her that we're divorced and besides that, I don't believe in the bible anymore. We have Christian neighbours who are always trying to turn me into a Christian, so I get exasperated at anyone trying to impose religion on me.

THAT SUMMER ANITA'S TWO boys stay with us for a couple of weeks. On the day I'm to take them home, the older one remembers that he left his T-shirt at the water hole. Debbie volunteers to go get it. She returns, covered in dirt and bruises. She tells me Paco attacked her. I rush her to the hospital. She has a hairline fracture along her jawbone. Later she tells us that the colt had picked her up and swung her around. She got loose by pinching his nose.

EARLY ONE MORNING I find our cat dead on the front lawn. It doesn't look like the dogs mauled her — they have all been living together peacefully. A few mornings later I find Saber having severe convulsions, so I take him to the vet. He'd been poisoned, probably with strychnine, which can cause brain damage. I take him back home, but the convulsions come again. I decide he has to be put down. I also take Dusty to the Winnipeg Humane Society. All the way to Winnipeg, he looks up at me with loving eyes. All the way back to the farm, I cry. We have one neighbour who is very strange and I think she is the one who is poisoning our animals.

ON AUGUST 28TH, 1980, I call Kathy to wish her happy birthday. She doesn't seem very happy and I end the conversation by telling her that I love her — that we all love her.

On October 6th, Kathy's husband calls to say Kathy has passed away. She started her car in the closed garage and died of carbon monoxide poisoning. Like Vivian, Kathy has committed suicide.

part three

Come
Walk
With Me

OCTOBER 1980 TO
OCTOBER 1987

INTERVIEW PART THREE

I GOT INVOLVED WITH A, with a real gentleman. He was a Polish guy. He was taken as a prisoner of war. He was there at that concentration camp for three years. And then when the war was over, he asked to come to Canada. And I met him here in Winnipeg. His name was Pete Poponiak. Yeah, he was very good to me. And he was always working. I never had to worry about nothing, with that guy. He had a place there, at Hadashville.

You know what he even done? He even told at the hotel there, "Whenever she wants beer, give it to her on credit. And I'll pay it."

My son, when he was going on 17, eh, he come and found me at Hadashville. A bunch of them were cadets, for a forester. Them boys used to go around, eh, learning the trees and stuff like that.

I don't know if he's still alive or what. I dream sometimes of, uh, my son. But, when he was small. Yeah. God only knows if I'll ever see him ….

When Kathy was small, she was only 11 years of age, and she win the first prize, for Red River jig. And I tell you I was a proud mother. We went to that violin contest with her in Winnipeg. At St. Vital. Yeah. And Andy Desjarlais was so proud of Kathy. And he said, "I'm so glad that half-breeds win." Cause he was a half-breed himself.

Pete Poponiak worked all the time, that guy. He even worked at Falcon Lake, at the motel, the two of us. We had a room there and board. And then after that, he kept on working there, and I came into Winnipeg. His boss used to bring him once a week to come and pay for my rent and to see that I had enough to eat. And wherever we went, I was never short of anything. And I was never hungry with him. I had lots of clothes. And I stayed with that guy for seven years.

And then, that guy and his partner, they were in the camps, cutting wood, cordwood and they had their own little camp, eh. And both of them burned to death, right in there. That's how I lost him. Yeah. After that, I came back to Winnipeg.

Oh yeah, that's the time I had a job as a nurse's aide. And while I was working there, that's the time, uh, Vivian drowned herself. The police come and told me. The RCMP told me that I have to go to Toronto and identify my daughter. And I went over there and I buried her. I was supposed to come right after the funeral, eh, back to my job. But over there, Kathy kept me for a week.

That's the time she was in the hospital. She pretty near got that, uh, that T.B. Yeah. Well, they let her out, eh, for the funeral. But she never went back again. Her doctor told her she didn't have to go back, gave her a big jar of pills. And they told her to come in and have check-ups.

And me, I came back. I went back to work. All I could do is two weeks, I worked, because I couldn't help myself. Specially one woman, one of my patients, Mrs. West, she used to tell me, "Clara, pray to God Jesus so that Jesus can take me too, just like he done with your daughter." I just had to run into the bathroom and cry there. And the head nurse said to me, "I don't think you'll be able to work no more." And then she gave me a letter, how I worked, to my doctor in St. Boniface — to give that letter to them. And that's what they told me, them doctors: "You cannot work no more. You're finished." It was just like a shock to me, when they come and told me that. But they told me, "You're in a good hands, with us here, you're in a good hands."

After that, the doctors told me, "You cannot be alone. Stay with your friends." And they gave me some pills, eh. And then they told me I had to go every week to go and see them. It was the doctors that put me on welfare. I was on welfare.

I went to visit Kathy in Toronto. That was the last time I seen her. I stayed in Toronto, seven months. You see, she was working and her husband had his own factory to go to. And the two little girls had to go to school. Then I wouldn't have nobody to stay with me. So she used to take me to my cousin Adeline's place. That's where I stayed mostly. And then she'd come and get me Friday nights to go and stay with them till Sunday nights.

Now, I got a nice place. It's in the highrise. It's a, how would you call that place? Senior home. Yeah. I cook for myself. I look after myself. I got good friends in there. Yeah. And they all tell me that, "Oh you're always clean, nice and clean. Your hair is always nicely combed."

Oh sure, sometimes if my friends comes, eh, we have a little, uh, a little party. Well, when I went and asked for that place, eh, they told me, "You can have a little party there."

Then I asked them, "Can my sister come and sleep with me when she comes in from out of the country? And when she comes in to see the doctor, can she come and stay with me?" "Oh sure," they told me that. Sure I can have people to come and visit me, and a little party we have, every once in a while. Now that I can't work no place, that's all I've got to do. But when you're getting old, you can't handle your liquor. You can just take so much, that's it. Yeah.

Oh, sometimes I got visitors, eh, who come to visit me. And I go out and visit them. My husband, he used to come and visit me. But he doesn't come and visit me now. Yeah, I see him sometimes at the Bingo, with that woman. And one time, we, uh, I was asked to go for dinner, eh, at the Indian Friendship Centre. And that's where I seen him again, with that same woman. I don't know her. But he hardly talks to me. Me, I don't care. He can have that woman. As long as she treats him good, that's all I'm asking. She looks after him really good, I'm happy. Oh yeah. He's still in my heart.

And I don't think I'll move away. I don't like moving. They always ask me, the caretakers in there and that lady that looks after us, they always ask me, "How do you like your little place? Do you still like it?"

"Oh, yes!" I said. I even signed papers to stay there for another year.

— *MARY CLARA PELLETIER MOSIONIER*

CHAPTER 16

LONG AFTER I HANG UP THE PHONE, I just sit there. Two trains of thought come to me almost simultaneously. They are so contradictory that I almost feel like two people.

First I realize that I had this same reaction to news of Vivian's death: no tears. Maybe I didn't love Kathy. Since I only got to know her as an adult, maybe we were more friends than sisters. I would probably never have seen her again, even if she were alive, so if she chose to take her life, why should I cry for her? Why should I miss her? If I went to her funeral, wouldn't that be just for show? When I recently assured her that I loved her, it was to make her feel good. I had added that we all loved her to diminish my responsibility, because I wasn't sure if I did love her. She must have sensed my doubt because people had lied to her before and she would have developed radar against lies.

The contradictory thought that comes is that I do love Kathy. The unconditional love I have for my children, and now Kathy, expands to include Vivian, Eddie, and my parents. I can love! And I do — and I suddenly know who I am.

I am the one with special insight. I am the one who was given three guardian animals to guide me. I am Métis. Everything in my childhood, everything in my past has happened so I could come to this moment. I can wallow in self-pity or I can do the special thing that I was meant to do.

So what is that special something? It has to be figuring out the whys. Why did my sisters kill themselves? Why were my parents alcoholics? Why did we grow up in white foster homes? Why is there racism? Why?

As I think about these questions, anger builds in me: first Vivian, now Kathy. I will have to figure out the answers and write them down. That's what I have to do: I have to write a book.

Whoa! I can't write a book. I'm a bookkeeper. I've never written anything except letters at the convent, and one-page letters to Bill. Those were just to pass the time, or exchange information, certainly not from a love of writing. But the idea sticks. I ask Linda to look after Billy and Debbie until Bill gets home, and I book a flight to Toronto.

I HAVE NO IDEA where Mom and Dad are living. In a way I'm grateful because I don't want to be the one to tell them of Kathy's death, even though they should be told. All I know of Eddie is that he is probably somewhere in British Columbia. The last time I was in touch with Dad or Eddie's friends, Garry and Lloyd, was back in 1967, so I don't know how to find any of them and don't have time before my flight. Maybe when I come back from Kathy's funeral, I can figure something out.

FOR SOME REASON, my flight lands in Ottawa, instead of Toronto. One of the other passengers says he's renting a car to drive to Toronto. Would I like a ride? Of course, I would. I need to get to Ajax. I assume he's asked others, but it's just the two of us on the drive. I tell him I'm going to my sister's funeral and that I'm going to write a book. It's the first time I say this out loud. He turns out to be a magazine editor and suggests that, as I've never written before, I write a story and he'll look it over for me. He drives me to Kathy's house in Ajax. I'm grateful for both the ride and his encouragement.

AT THE FUNERAL I keep wondering why Kathy would go into their garage, turn on the car, and let carbon monoxide put her to sleep. She has two beautiful daughters and a lovely house close to Lake Ontario. She and her husband have decent jobs and a lot of friends. She had it all. Didn't she?

At the house her husband shows me a small piece of paper torn from a brown paper lunch bag. They had found it on the kitchen counter. The only thing written on it is, "I'm sorry." He gives me a few keepsakes, among them a pink wallet containing a newspaper clipping of Vivian's suicide.

I RETURN TO VITA in time for Billy's birthday and we buy Debbie a special present for her birthday. At the end of the month Bill misses Debbie's birthday because he has to be on the road. Debbie is so delighted with her brand new bicycle that I keep it in the kitchen near the back door just so she can look at it until Bill gets home. Then he'll store it in the basement over winter.

The day after Debbie's birthday I catch up with the bookkeeping for Bill's business. That night Billy and Debbie are in the living room watching TV while I make supper. Billy notices light dancing on the staircase wall and I go upstairs to see what it is.

Debbie's room is on fire!

I race down the stairs and tell the kids to get out of the house. Billy takes Debbie's new bicycle out the back door and she follows with Lady in her arms. Although the fire is confined to Debbie's room, I know the first rule is to get out. I don't even think of trying to put the fire out. Once Billy and Debbie are safely outside, the bookkeeper in me wants to grab the bookkeeping files — how could I do taxes without them? Instead I open the top drawer and, seeing Kathy's wallet and a file containing certificates and mementoes, I grab them instead and join the kids. By the time the fire truck comes, our house is engulfed in flames and, mindless of all the people who have gathered, I cry for the loss of the things that can't be replaced: the pictures of Debbie and Billy's early years, and the keepsakes from Kathy's family.

I don't remember where we went that night. I imagine I drove us to Anita's place in Transcona. Days later, when Tanya learns of the fire, she collects clothing, mostly for the kids. I am so grateful to her, especially since she is also dealing with the death of someone close to her. In the following weeks we have to move the animals to a neighbour's farm, where they will be looked after.

With all the upheaval, I forget to try to find my parents.

WE FIND AN AFFORDABLE house in Oakbank, about 20 minutes east of Transcona, but we keep the farmland. In March after I finish our taxes, I buy a typewriter, write an Alfred Hitchcock tongue-in-cheek story, and send it to the editor in Toronto. When I receive a reply that my writing needs editing but is saleable, I begin thinking seriously about my book-to-be.

What makes me think I could write a book? Well, over the years I've read a lot of books about a lot of different things: animal stories, Louis L'Amour westerns, biographies, histories of other countries, murder mysteries galore, ghost stories. If I love certain authors' books, I'll try to read all their other books. Sometimes I go to garage sales and I'm ecstatic when I can come home with boxes of books. Bill thinks I'm super smart because I know things that other people don't. Then there's that composition from grade 6. Since then, compositions have been easy for me. And a book would be like writing composition after composition.

I've begun to watch such shows as *Woodsmoke & Sweetgrass*, in which Sherry Theobald interviews people, most of whom are Native. I collect articles, letters to the editor, and editorials from newspapers and magazines when they are about Native people. And I read a few more books that are like Heather Robertson's *Reservations Are for Indians*, which Linda had given me. If some of the articles, letters, and editorials are not complimentary to Native people — most suggest they get too much funding and squander taxpayers' money — I try to see beneath the surface. Why are Native people so poor and why are they so scrutinized? Journalists seemed to have no idea or interest in the causes of the "Native problems" on which they reported. This angers me and makes me even more determined. If I'm going to turn trees into book pages, then those pages had better be meaningful.

I decide to write about two Métis sisters: one fair-skinned and one brown like me. That way I can represent a white and an Indian point of view. I'll write it as fiction in the third person. If I get the answers

I'm looking for, I will want to have the book published. But then I think: who would read a book about Métis sisters? Only Métis women. Well, I could go on and on like that and never get to the writing, so I stop with the speculations.

I pick the name April for my main character because I've always loved that name. The reason I didn't give that name to Debbie was because she was born in October. April represents springtime to me, when new life begins. There are no Raintrees in the phone book and I want a name that's unique. Also, Raintree has an Indian flavour and sounds perfect. I pick the name Cheryl for the sister because it reminds me of *cherie* in French. I want her to be the loveable sister, like Vivian.

Starting with April's birth, I plot a timeline on graph paper. April will be the older sister, about my age, so I can use events from my life to make her life sound real. She will represent all the times I wished I could pass for white. Cheryl will be brown-skinned, representing my childhood years when I was pleased to have Indian blood. My parents are alcoholics, so April and Cheryl's parents have to be alcoholics.

Like us, the girls would be placed in foster homes by Children's Aid, when April is about five and Cheryl about three. While mine were pretty good foster homes, bad things happened to me. I didn't know if similar bad things happened to my brother and sisters. Regardless, over the years I've noticed that former foster children have a reputation that makes others wary of them. In television shows if they need a mentally unbalanced criminal or deranged killer or drug addict, that character usually comes from a foster home.

My characters will experience racism: Cheryl will be on the receiving end; and April, who can pass for white, will deliver some of it, unintentionally. April will marry a rich white man from Toronto and move there, thinking she can escape the "problem" of her heritage. When she is back in Winnipeg, racist men will rape her. In the aftermath she will be oblivious to Cheryl's downward spiral. Cheryl's suicide will force her to make a choice: perpetual self-pity or self-acclamation.

I won't include their childhood years because readers might think this fictional account is based on my own parents and my real foster homes, and they might make wrong assumptions and judgments.

Both sisters will be beautiful and highly intelligent. Cheryl will go to university, and be outspoken or sassy when needed. April will use her beauty to marry into wealth and, although she'll be divorced, she will be free from financial worries. This is so the bookkeeper in me doesn't get bogged down with finances.

One problem: since I'm writing in the third person and Cheryl is to become a heavy drinker, I'll need to learn more about alcoholism. Although I have been to bars in my younger days, I've always tried to avoid those who drink too much. Except for the brief time that Mom lived with us, I can't remember seeing anyone close to me drunk. Bill and I are coffee drinkers. Could I learn from books, or do I have to go bar-hopping? Whatever I do, Cheryl's alcoholism will have to be believable.

WHEN BILL IS ON the road, I get up to give the kids breakfast and see them off to school, then go back to bed until they are due home for lunch. When they go back to school for the afternoon, I begin typing at the dining room table. I stop when they come home and start again once they're in bed. Then I work till about four or five in the morning and sleep until it's time to get up for the kids. If Bill is home, I don't write. As the kitchen, dining room, and living room are open, anyone in this area would keep me from concentrating. I can clear away my type-writer and papers, though it's harder to clear my mind. My notepads are scattered around for when ideas or a new scene comes to mind and sometimes Bill thinks I'm angry because I don't talk to him.

Writing is kind of fun, especially when the characters do their own thing and don't follow my outline. Then one night at 3 a.m., when I'm almost finished the first draft, an essay comes to me. It's as if someone is dictating and I type as fast as I can to keep up. When the essay seems finished, I just sit there, wondering. The prose is not mine. Where did it come from? A spirit world? My animal guides? Who knows — it's here and needs a place in my story.

The essay summarizes five hundred years of Indian history, from first contact with Europeans. It tells of white oppression of Indian nations and of Mother Earth. It also summarizes my feelings and thoughts, instinctive and learned, about how the land, the waters, the air, the animals, and the people have been contaminated by greed and disrespect.

I want to give the essay to April, the survivor; but it belongs to Cheryl's character, as she's the one who values her Indian heritage. It will also show that Cheryl is the thinker, trying to make April see the Indian point of view. It belongs in an Indian setting so I send the sisters off to a powwow. Since I have never been to one I can only imagine what it's like, and later when I do go, I can fill out the setting and circumstances.

MURRAY SINCLAIR, a lawyer, has agreed to give me advice on the rape trial scene of my novel. Like me, he's Native. Unlike me, he has a powerful presence that comes from traditional knowledge. I'm compelled to confide in him what I have never told anyone, not even my brother: I have three animal guardians — the wolf, the cougar, and the bear. I tell him this right up front, and wait. I have no traditional knowledge, only childhood instincts. Will he think I'm daft and send me on my way? Will he think I'm so weak that I need three such animals?

What he does is validate my childhood instincts by telling me about his spirit animal. I sit there, amazed: I'm not alone! How did I get the instinct that made me aware of my animal guardians? I'm not even a full-blooded Indian. Do white people ever have guardian animals?

AT THE END OF April 1981 what I've typed on my cheap canary-yellow paper is a fairly good story. I've cut and taped rewrites to the appropriate pages, and other pages have large portions x-ed out, all in an effort to conserve paper. When I re-read it all, parts make me think of Harlequin romances, and while I've read and enjoyed them, I don't want that for this book. Perhaps I've concentrated too much on April's romances, first with her husband to-be and later with the lawyer at work who becomes her sounding board. As for my dialogue — and, well, everything else — I need a professional Native writer to help me make it publishable. With that in mind, I look for a Native publisher.

I phone the Manitoba Métis Federation, or MMF, and ask if they know of any Native publishers, expecting a flat no. Instead they tell me about Pemmican Publications, which started in October 1980. Kathy died that month and this publishing house was born. Maybe they are meant to publish my novel.

CHAPTER 17

D EBBIE, BILLY, AND BILL ALL MISS Vita, so in the summer of 1981, we sell the Oakbank house, buy a large mobile home, and move back to the farm. Summer holidays go by quickly, what with all the details of moving and being back in the fields on the tractor, cutting and raking. In the fall we'll be baling and stacking. The one thing we don't need to do anymore is gather wood.

IN MAY I HAD taken my cut-and-paste manuscript to Pemmican Publications and told them I was hoping to work with a professional writer. In September I hear from Virginia Maracle at Pemmican. They want to publish my book. Could I come in for an appointment with Dorine Thomas, the managing editor?

At our meeting, Dorine tells me to re-write my manuscript without looking at my first draft and doesn't mention a co-writer. She gives me a few Pemmican books about Métis history. The book, *The Métis: Canada's Forgotten People*, by D. Bruce Sealey and Antoine S. Lussier, is especially informative. (It opens asking when the Métis nation originated. The standard answer is, "Nine months after the first White man set foot in Canada.") She also suggests that I read *The Diviners*, by Margaret Laurence, and *Half-Breed*, by Maria Campbell, which I begin reading as soon as I get home. I figure Pemmican might approach Maria Campbell to work with me, so I make only half-hearted attempts to re-write my manuscript.

AT THE BEGINNING of January I get severe stomach pains. I've had them before, and twice went to emergency, but the doctors said I just had a stomach flu and sent me home. This time we go to the doctor in Vita who discovers I have gallstones. Within a week I'm in St. Boniface Hospital. Once back home it takes me until spring to feel ready to write again.

IN MY NOVEL I really want to show the humour I shared with my foster sisters and with Eddie and his friends, but I haven't been able to. We laughed so much, although I can't remember any of the Chevaliers laughing, and now I think the humour was one of our survival mechanisms. I wonder, though, with the rape and Cheryl's alcoholism and suicide, if there's any room for humour. Dorine suggests that I write in the first person, a really good piece of advice. Maybe using April's voice will allow for some lightheartedness.

In using her voice, one problem will be solved. She'll know as much as I do about alcoholism. However another problem crops up. How will she know of Cheryl's lifestyle when they are apart? Well, I'm confident that the solution will come.

ONE AFTERNOON DEBBIE AND I are sitting at the table having a snack and she says, "Mom, you have a grey hair. Do you want me to pull it out?"

I reply, "No. They say that for every grey hair you pull out, seven more will grow in."

She thinks about this for a few seconds and then asks, "Well, why don't you pull out some black hairs?"

That makes me chuckle; but later it occurs to me that I can use that simple logic with April and Cheryl as children. Everything is new and fresh to them. I was a lot smarter when I was very young. As I got older I stopped using my instincts and my ability to see things with simplicity. Yes, I do need to write in their childhood years.

IN MY PREVIOUS DRAFT I had written about "cunning trickery" instinctively, as I knew nothing about Native politics. Since the end of 1980, I have been learning.

Why did alcohol and suicide destroy our family? I think it started long before our time. I think it started when Indian leaders, given their oral histories, signed treaties with the Canadian government, which wrote everything down. The witnesses and translators were often priests. When I observed the hypocrisy of the priest who turned away the woman and her children from Catechism classes and experienced the corruption of the priest who molested me, I now have a difficult time believing priests are credible. How hard would it have been for them to get someone who can't read to sign documents with an *X*? Apparently, those treaty documents can be interpreted to mean many things. Indian leaders thought they would be sharing the land with the white man and going about their own business. Instead the government sent them to reserves, on land ill-suited to agriculture, and left them there to figure out how to farm.

Indian leaders requested that schools be built on these reserves. Instead distant church-run residential schools were built, to where Indian children were taken to assimilate, as set out in the Indian Act. If, in time, there were no more Indians, the treaties would become obsolete. My white side could be very cunning.

How do I begin my book? Well, the first word that comes to me is: "Memories." Not just April's memories — collective memories, distant memories, spiritual memories that can never die.

As some Métis people also experienced residential schools — Mom had been in the Camperville and Lebret schools — so will Alice Raintree, April and Cheryl's mother. She will be taught how to speak English and how to do menial work, but little else. As for life skills, she and her husband, Henry, learn only to "medicate" themselves with alcohol.

Later, residential schools are replaced by the provincially controlled child-welfare system. It perpetuates the same treatment of and the long-term effects on many of the children, as the residential school system did.

I need a scene of April and Cheryl being taken from their home so that readers will know how generations of Native children and parents felt when the system splits families apart. I begin with, "Our free idle days with our family came to an end one summer afternoon." The rest pours out in a gush of emotions that has me crying, as I think of the children who must have been so excited to go for that airplane ride, never knowing where they would end up.

Although the Dions, April's first foster family, are well-intentioned, they are a part of the assimilation process: let Native children see what they can have with us and they will be happy to abandon what they had. It worked on me. It will work on April. But it will not work on Cheryl.

Young Cheryl nicknames April, "Apple." It is only later that I'm reminded of Eddie telling me that he saw Kathy, Vivian, and me as "apples." It strikes me as ironic that I chose the name April, which lends itself to the nickname, Apple.

As a teenager and an adult, I had made no conscious decision to live like a white person. I just came to accept the values of the dominant society. My spirituality was buried under Catholic teachings. My animal guardians were forgotten.

My next family for April is the 'Indian agent,' Mrs. DeRosier. The government appointed white men to be Indian agents, authorizing them to maintain dictatorial control on reserves. Cheryl will be my spokesperson for that history lesson in grade 5 that had such a negative impact on me.

The DeRosier family makes me so angry that I create a scene in which April can beat the living daylights out of the nasty DeRosier kids. I write about the unspoken, stereotypical expectations I perceived in my childhood and call it the "Native girl" syndrome. Many children meet the expectations, good or bad, placed on them. By the time I went out on my own I thought I had no ambition; but in rethinking this for the novel, I realize I did have one ambition — not to end up on skid row.

Ironies come to me as I'm writing the syndrome scene. Eddie and I were obedient, well-behaved children when we were taken into foster care. Kathy ran away not to some boyfriend but to go back to Mom and Dad. Mrs. Chevalier was upset when Vivian moved away. Eddie lived in the same foster home until he went out on his own, so his foster mother must have been happy with him. If my parents were such a mess that we had to be taken away, then who taught us to be such well-behaved children? Did we really have to be taken? Well, if cunning trickery was to work, then yes, we did have to be taken.

By the time April is no longer a foster child, she is assimilated, as intended. She perceives Native people as most of Canadian society sees them and, as intended, wants no part of them.

This is where the second draft joins the first. I edit out much of April's relationships with Bob Radcliff and Roger Madison and remove Cheryl's activities when she's not with April. I still have to figure out a way for April to learn of these activities later.

WHEN I COME TO THE RAPE, I realize why I chose it over child molestation. The rape of April is that of Native people worldwide, where dominant societies destroy a way of life through their oppression. When the rapist tells April that she likes being raped, he represents the oppressor. This is what forced assimilation feels like. When he pisses in her mouth, he is letting her know that he has no respect for her body and soul, just as oppressors have no respect for the land they rape for diamonds and oil. This is what it feels like.

IN THE SUMMER OF 1982, I go to my first powwow with Debbie. I am so shy, as I don't know what to expect. I'm not sure if we'll even be welcome because we're not Treaty; but then I see white people being let in. In one area, numerous display booths have been set up with Native items for sale. Groups of teenage girls in traditional dress walk by, talking and laughing, the bells on their clothing jingling with each step. Older women, looking serene and content, look at the displays of jewellery and crafts. Many of them are also in traditional clothing and wear bold-coloured shawls. The men with painted faces are the most colourfully dressed, in furs, feathers, or leather.

When the dancing begins, everyone is invited to join in and some white visitors enthusiastically take part. I know there's a reason for everything in Indian traditions but I can only watch as an outsider. The drumming gets into my blood and I am drawn into the beats, thinking how happy these people look. They have been through harsh times, yet here they are, celebrating life. I am so proud of them. I am so proud that part of me comes from them. And my tears are of joy and acknowledgment. This unexpected emotion, this reclaiming what I had rejected, is what I need to give to April.

She and I will never again feel a need to apologize for the "drunken Natives on Main Street." We are part of those people as much as we are part of the people at this powwow, even though I know none of them. The shame I was made to feel of being part Indian remained with me far too long.

My RAGE WHEN I was a teenager came from a subconscious awareness that great social injustices were being done to Native people. I couldn't identify it back then, but it surfaces as I'm thinking about Cheryl. At times, the blame for my rage had fallen on the victims, as the word, *oppressor,* had never been uttered in my schooling. Cheryl will see what most Canadians don't see, such as enormous government subsidies to exploitive businesses slipping by almost unnoticed, while politicians publicize every cent of taxpayers' money that goes to Native people.

Having realized that Native peoples would not disappear, the government ensured that their voices would be drowned out by their own voice of propaganda. The parts of the treaties that benefited the governments were quickly settled, but not those that might benefit the Indian nations.

Big oil companies, mining companies, forestry industries, and hydro projects could pilfer from those Native territorial lands, where treaty commitments had not been fulfilled. Their profits are stolen. An economy based on such corruption, such thievery, makes accomplices of us all.

This is Cheryl's knowledge. It's the basis of her essay at the powwow. It's the foundation of her disgust with April in her last drunken rage: "...Your white governments, your white churches, sitting back in idle rich comfort, preaching what ought to be but making sure it isn't."

FOR APRIL TO DISCOVER what Cheryl was doing when they weren't connected, I create Cheryl's journals. Her voice will contrast with April's mostly flat account of their lives. When people tell me stories of harsh treatment, the way they tell it gives it credibility. Those stories told genuinely in monotone have more emotional impact on me than a flamboyant style would.

IN SURVIVING AS A Métis woman, April will embrace her Indian spirituality. This is the source of Native strength that the churches and governments had tried to suppress, the power that survives imposed religion, the power that sustains the Indian spirit against all odds. In the novel, I write words that promise hope — and the child, Henry Liberty Raintree, is part of that hope for April. As I'm not sure which teachings and traditions are to be shared with the public, I write only what spirituality means to me.

Indian spirituality means that we look at things as a whole rather than in bits and pieces.

We are a part of Mother Earth, just as the land and the animals and the waters and the air are.

We harvest in a way that allows for the renewal and the continuation of life.

We nurture our young so they may play and learn and embrace life-long learning.

We recognize that we need to adapt to the cycles of change.

We treat each other and all living things with dignity and respect.

We recognize and respect that other races have their beliefs and religions and cultural traditions, just as we do.

Indian spirituality is a way of life that should be with us at all times.

CHAPTER 18

NOW THAT I'VE LEARNED A BIT MORE of what publishers expect, I'm amazed that my first mess of pages was even read. My second draft is typed, double-spaced, on white paper with the required margins, all nice and neat. I mail it to Pemmican Publications. However, Dorine has left and I'm wondering if the new managing editor, Ray Unger, will like my manuscript. Maybe it won't get published after all.

In September shortly after Bill gets notice that he is being laid off, Virginia calls. Pemmican Publications is still planning to publish my book, and what's of more interest to me right now is that there's a job opening. I apply and Ray hires me.

WE PUT THE VITA FARM up for sale and begin packing. Bill finds a large house to rent in Winnipeg and takes me to see it. As soon as the landlord sees me, he suddenly remembers he has just rented it. I'm hurt and angry at his obvious racism. Suspecting we'll have a very hard time renting, I look in the "for sale" columns.

I find a townhouse in St. Norbert and qualify to assume the mortgage. It's ironic to be back in St. Norbert. After the first time I left, I used to have recurring dreams that I was leaving St. Norbert and a mummy was chasing the bus. It was coming for me, and it wanted to keep me from leaving. I had always awoken before the mummy got to me. Those dreams made me feel that I had 'escaped' St. Norbert and I would never return to live there.

In October we move. Debbie attends a nearby elementary school and Billy has to go to my old high school. Debbie is quick to make new friends, but Billy never brings friends home, which is new for him. He will later tell me that racism was still alive and well at the school. At the time he doesn't say anything, keeping it inside, as I had done. I can only sense there's some problem, other than wanting to be back in Vita and I conclude that he must blame me for the move. Bill has found work for his rig with another trucking company and is often away on the road.

PEMMICAN PUBLICATIONS is a non-profit publisher, whose mandate is to educate the Métis people about their history and culture. The founders had a five-year funding commitment under the Local Employment Assistance Program (LEAP). Their office is on the ground floor of a huge house on Carlton Street and it's very impressive. They even have their own typesetting equipment and a fully equipped darkroom since they also publish a quarterly journal. Because it has not made a profit and is not likely to become self-supporting, Pemmican is seen as a white elephant, and LEAP officials decide to end their funding in June 1983 instead of in October 1985.

My new job is to sell advertising for the journal and to promote Pemmican's books. One of my assignments is to go to Toronto to meet with the three big book retailers at the time — Coles, W.H. Smith, and Classics. As I have no idea that these three are a big deal to Canadian publishers, I'm not intimidated as I call them to make appointments. Virginia has to lend me some of her business suits for the trip because my wardrobe consists of jeans and pullovers. In Toronto I can't tell whether the book buyers are interested or just being polite to an amateur. We'll find out if they order any books.

I SEND LETTERS TO Maria Campbell, Margaret Laurence, Farley Mowat, and Ray Torgrud, a thoughtful and gentle Winnipeg TV talk-show host, asking them to write blurbs for my book. Only Farley Mowat declines, as he is in the middle of his own writing and doesn't have time. Maria

Campbell responds with a great letter that I don't want shortened, so I ask the managing editor to include it in the book. Ray Torgrud and Margaret Laurence write fantastic blurbs.

THAT CHRISTMAS OF 1982 we have Bill's family over for Christmas dinner. Some of them think I must be excited that my book is about to be published. I'm not. For one thing the book, though fictional, comes from the tragedies that my family and I faced. I also had to argue with Ray Unger, first, not to change the final title I chose, *In Search of April Raintree*, and then to change some of the terms in my contract. I hate arguing and will try to avoid it any way that I can.

One of the Christmas presents Bill got for the kids is an Atari Pac Man and I'm the one who plays with it the most. On weekend mornings I get up very early and play at the beginner's level, so I can get lots of points. It's a great stress reliever. What's bothering me is that Pemmican will probably go out of business without the LEAP funding, taking both my job and my book with it. In my contract, I've made it easy for another publisher to be able to publish my book, but which one would want to?

RAY HIRES AN ARTIST to do watercolour paintings for the book cover, none of which I like. They are too busy. Then one day on the drafting table, a reverse photo, white on black, catches my eye. I tell Ray I like that effect. With some whiteout ink, he makes a design on black paper of a coffee cup — because I'm always drinking coffee — and two feathers, one up, one down. I like it. For me its stark simplicity represents the text.

AN EXCERPT FROM my novel is published in *The Pemmican Journal*. In British Columbia, Eddie sees it and writes to me at Pemmican. I write back to let him know about Kathy. I had last seen Eddie in 1969 and, except for a couple of letters afterwards, we hadn't been in contact. He moved, I moved, and we lost touch. When he gets my letter, he calls, and we talk for quite a while. He tells me I should not use the word "Native" because that's the word the government uses for us. He is tremendously pleased that his little sister has written a book and is looking forward to reading it.

I FIND MYSELF IN another argument with Ray over his editing changes. Despite my objections, he typesets the manuscript as edited and prepares it for the printer. (I guess it wasn't really an argument.) The preparation is a labour-intensive process at the time, both tedious and time-consuming.

To be fair, many of his changes are good, but some have changed the beat, which he doesn't consider important. Composing the words is musical in a way I can't explain. It's instinctive. He has also lost some of the Indian voice of Cheryl's essay, and I feel a very strong need to protect this passage because of the way it came to me.

Once the manuscript has been typeset, it becomes my job to catch mistakes in the proofs. I begin quite focused; but soon I'm engaged in the story and forget to proofread. I imagine the first few pages of any book are without errors.

When Virginia sees how upset I am over some of Ray's changes, she tells me we can stay late and she will reset the parts I don't like. The technology of that time demands that what I rewrite take up exactly the same space as the lines we are replacing. The next morning my manuscript goes off to the printers, with Ray none the wiser. It is to be in mass-market format. Ray had wanted to print 10,000 copies but one of Pemmican's funders has insisted on 5,000 maximum.

In early March, while the book-to-be is at the printers, Ray decides to leave Pemmican at the beginning of May. He asks if I want to take over as the managing editor. I ask Virginia if she wants the job because she has been there from the beginning. When she says no, I accept, even though I have no idea what his job entails. I'm interviewed and approved by the MMF board of directors and they decide I'll do, mostly because no one else is available.

In April 1983, *In Search of April Raintree* is published.

CHAPTER 19

THE TWO FIRST BUYERS OF MY BOOK are Gerald Monette, president of Turtle Mountain Community College, and John C. Crawford, professor of linguistics at the University of North Dakota. When the boxes of books arrive from the printer, both are at Pemmican to discuss publishing details for *The Michif Dictionary, Turtle Mountain Chippewa Cree*, being edited by Mr. Crawford. As far as I know, no one but Pemmican staff members has read my book. Now I'm wondering how these two scholarly men are going to like my little book.

After work, Virginia and I celebrate by going to the BBQ Restaurant for coffee and banana cream pie — I just love their banana cream pie! I still feel no big excitement in being a "published author," because we don't know if Pemmican will survive.

A VOLUNTEER FROM THE FRIENDSHIP Centre reads that I am the daughter of Louis and Mary Clara Mosionier and she lets me know that they are both living in Winnipeg. From this time on I always know where they live, Mom on Dufferin Avenue and Dad on Isabel Street, and I visit them often. Eventually I talk to each of them about my book. It's important that they know that the characters are fictional. I ask if I can talk publicly about their drinking when we kids were in foster care. Both agree — Mom says that whatever will help others will be good.

Later I realize they both seemed to know of Kathy's death. I rack my brain trying to figure out how they might have learned this. Was it from my book? If so, what a horrible way to find out that you lost a child! On the other hand, maybe Auntie Ada told them. But no, she may not even have known because she wasn't at the funeral. I don't even know where she was at the time, and still don't. If they did learn it from my book, I suddenly regret having it published. Yet, if I hadn't, I might never have been reunited with them, and Eddie and I wouldn't have been in touch again.

At one of our visits, Mom tells me of a humorous incident when Eddie and I still lived at home. Our Auntie Elsie was going with a black man named Charlie. Elsie stayed over one Saturday night. Early the next morning Mom and Elsie awoke, and from the bedroom they could hear the sound of a kitchen chair being scraped back and forth on the kitchen floor, so they finally got up to investigate. There we were, dressed in our Sunday best, but Sonny had found the black shoe polish. We were trying to make the white kitchen chairs black and we had also smeared the polish on our good clothes, and all over our arms, hands, and faces. As Mom stood in the doorway dismayed by the mess we had made, Elsie piped up, "I guess they want to be black like Charlie." With that, Mom just burst out laughing.

She told me that another time we lived in a three-storey house. The third-floor window frame had no window. Mom was in the front yard talking to a neighbour and she heard me shout, "Mommy, look at me." She couldn't see me until I shouted again from high up. When she saw me standing in the window opening she said her heart just about stopped. She told me not to move and ran inside and up those stairs. She got me back into the room safely. When she tells me about this, I recall the bedpan disaster in the hospital and wonder now if this incident had anything to do with my ingrained obedience.

I never asked her about the bad times, although she knew that if she wanted to talk about them, I was willing to listen. I didn't tell her about being molested either — adding to her painful memories seemed cruel. She did tell me about one of the times she and Dad went to court to try to get us kids back. The judge sat high on the bench looking down on them and the social workers and everybody in there were speaking against them. As Mom is recalling that time, she is trembling with remembered rage. "If I had a gun," she says, "I would have shot them all. Every last one of them."

I sit there quietly with tears in my eyes, remembering that I thought they had abandoned us and never did try to get us back. Filled with useless remorse, I silently make my apology to them: Oh, Mom, I didn't know any of this. I'm so sorry for the horrible thoughts I had about you and Dad. I'm so sorry that I gave up on you.

Up to that moment I had been visiting Mom mainly out of a sense of duty. Dad was the one who came to all the visits and to the receiving home. Ever since I got out of Children's Aid I've carried guilt for having rejected him. But I had never really forgiven Mom. Now listening to her anger and pain, I am filled with outrage by the racism they must have endured.

As a child and a teenager, I had felt unloved and unlovable. And now I learn that my parents had gone through such agony because they loved us after all. When we part that night we hug for a long time and I feel my mother's wet cheek against my face. I try to make her feel all the love and compassion that I had withheld for too many years.

In May Pemmican moves out of its beautiful spacious office to a quarter of the space in the MMF headquarters. Pemmican's accountant shows me that the *Pemmican Journal* has taken up most of the annual funding, despite its small subscription base. I decide to close it down and concentrate on publishing books. We ensure that all subscribers receive their refunds along with our book catalogue, so the mailing also serves as a promotional effort.

Virginia and I decide to publish more children's books. Native Studies courses are now offered at university levels; however, we also have to promote positive feelings at the elementary level. Because we have a niche market, I expand the bookkeeping system to track sales so we can target future marketing and promotion, and build networks with Native organizations. Virginia continues with the bookkeeping, while I apply for grants, and have Pemmican's contracts revised to benefit both the publisher and the author. We both work on production and she teaches me how to use the typesetting equipment.

Our first children's book is called *Nobody*. It's a delightful story about a mysterious trickster who does all the mischievous things that children might do if he weren't around. Then Keiron Guiboche walks in with cartoon drawings full of Métis humour. While a cartoon book was not on our menu, *Bufflo & Sprucegum* becomes our second book.

As we're building Pemmican's list, I'm also being asked to do local televised interviews, among them, *Woodsmoke & Sweetgrass* and the *Ray Torgrud Show*. I'm so nervous. I feel I don't know anything about anything — so what am I going to talk about? Then it comes to me: I need to make the interviewer look good. That means I have to talk, giving intelligent honest answers. (Intelligent? Well, I'll try.)

In Winnipeg I do enough television interviews that Virginia tells me that early one morning her nine-year-old daughter was flicking through the channels. When asked why, she replied that she was looking for Beatrice's show. I never watch or listen to my interviews; if I did, I would probably never do another one.

When I was writing the book, it never occurred to me that I would have to do media interviews or that I would be invited to do readings and talks. I feel so inadequate as a speaker that I never ask to be paid. My shyness is not the only factor. I also feel constricted by those things I can't talk about as I try to protect the privacy of those around me, mine included. Fortunately, organizations and libraries pay authors honorariums. I also use these speaking engagements to promote Pemmican Publications, and my novel helps open a lot of doors for Pemmican. (A friend tells Virginia of being on a northern flight, and all the passengers on the plane had their heads bent to read their copies of *In Search of April Raintree*.)

BECAUSE OF MY NOVEL, I've been invited to community meetings organized by the Winnipeg Coalition on Native Child Welfare, a coalition of urban Native organizations with a stake in child welfare. Chief Judge Edwin Kimelman tables what I think is an overly cautious report on the child-welfare system in Manitoba.

According to the Coalition, Native peoples had been denouncing the Children's Aid Society for years for its policy of out-of-province adoptions, and Native children have even been sent to the United States. This practice continued right up to 1982, when a moratorium was put in place. At the same time, the CAS was bypassing available Native foster homes.

Native parents had accused CAS of unfairly apprehending their children and of having no recourse. Yet Kimelman blames Native organizations for remaining silent too long before demanding control of their children, although he agrees with Native leaders that the child-welfare system had committed cultural genocide. The Coalition's mission is to provide a child and family services agency of our own, but Kimelman does not recommend "racially oriented" aid societies.

Under criticism and scrutiny, the Children's Aid Society of Winnipeg has decided to add more Native people to its current 32 board members, of whom only two are Native. It has sent invitations to three or four Native people to run in board elections. The Coalition plans to protest at the CAS general meeting, as this is an obvious attempt to window dress with 'token' Indians while changing little else.

Virginia and I get an invitation to the AGM luncheon, but I don't know if it's from the Coalition or the CAS. We find ourselves at a table of CAS social workers. Although I've written my novel, I'm still reluctant to be disloyal to the CAS. They had been there for me when I needed them. (It must be the Stockholm syndrome.) I listen to the talk around me: this one can't decide whether to go to Florida or Hawaii for a family vacation; that one can't decide which university to send his son to; and on it goes like that. It occurs to me that these people have no empathy for the people whose lives they control.

The Coalition files in and asks permission for Elijah Harper to speak. As he steps up to the mike, someone behind me mutters, "I wonder if he can even talk."

That does it — I know now where I belong. From that day on, I do whatever I can to support the Coalition.

AT THE END OF AUGUST Virginia and I attend a two-week book-publishing course at the Banff Arts Centre. During one of the sessions a guest lecturer from one of the large publishing houses recalls his days as a travelling sales representative. He was on a bus up north when a "drunken Indian" puked all over him. As the only two Native people in the room Virginia and I are in shock. The lecturer gets dead silence instead of the expected reaction but nobody speaks up. They probably don't know what to say to this unexpected insult, either.

At lunch I spot him at the end of the cafeteria line so I nudge Virginia to follow me and we get in line behind him. Unwilling to let his comment go, I say to Virginia, loud enough so he can hear, "Better watch what you eat, because you don't want to be puking all over him." He glances at us then stares straight ahead. I know I'm being petty but if he had apologized we'd have forgiven him then and there.

We learn so much from the rest of the course that it is worth both the overt and the subtle racism we encounter. Some people don't intend to be racist, and when they want to say something nice, they single out a positive trait of one Indian they know, implying that most Indians don't share this wonderful trait. What's that saying about good intentions?

At Banff I share a room with Pat Sanders, an editor from Turnstone Press in Winnipeg. One night when the course is almost over, we're sitting on our beds, just talking. Then she tells me she has been so overwhelmed by our quiet strength and dignity in dealing with the racism we've encountered that she couldn't bring herself to talk to me about it before this night. Her telling me this means a lot to me.

WE GET HOME FROM Banff on a Friday and the following Monday I'm off to Montreal, Ottawa, and Toronto for the first leg of my promotion tour. In Montreal I stay with Denise, Anita's sister. As a professional singer, she has often moved, as have I; and we hadn't seen each other since we were both pregnant more than 16 years earlier. In Ottawa, I stay at Jean Goodwill's place, and Norma Sluman comes over so we can discuss publishing matters for their book, *John Tootoosis*.

One of my Toronto interviews is with Peter Gzowski, who has a radio show called *Morningside*. I listen to the radio for music, never for talk shows, so I have no idea who Peter Gzowski is or how popular his show is until I get back to Winnipeg. Listeners from across Canada have sent letters and book orders because they heard me on *Morningside*.

AFTER BEING HOME for almost a week, I reluctantly head off on the western leg of my promotion tour. So far all the interviewers have been friendly and supportive so I'm jarred when one radio interviewer in Regina asks me why Native people insist on writing books designed to make white people feel guilty about the past. He adds that white people are sick and tired of it. I ask in turn what actions white people have taken to undo the injustices of the past? After the interview he tells me it will be edited for broadcast. I can only assume he will silence my voice. On my way out I question his attitude, for which he has no answer.

By now I'm already tired of airports and worrying about being on time for the next flight or the next interview. More than that, I'm disappointed in myself. I have all these chances to say something important and I always come away feeling that I missed an opportunity. Constrained by time and my shyness, I don't even try to connect my novel to our history or to why that history was thrust on us.

In Saskatoon, I confide in Maria Campbell about the self-doubts I have in doing this publicity stuff. She tells me I have a gift for writing and I need to share it with our people. And the publicity is the way to do it. I'm not so sure I have a gift because I've said all I have to say in this one book. I have no intention of writing more books. Nevertheless, I leave Saskatoon for Edmonton, determined to do the best I can. Maria has arranged for Tantoo Cardinal to take me around Edmonton. I am as impressed with her as I am with Maria.

In Calgary on an open-line radio talk show, the very first caller is an irate-sounding man who wants to know why Indians have all these treaty rights and can get free housing and free this and free that, while white people have to work hard all their lives. I have my theories but I don't have the expertise to answer to his tirade effectively. Fortunately a second caller gives an in-depth answer. After that the rest of the callers ask about my book and the balance of the show goes smoothly for me. The second caller has left her phone number and message with the switchboard for me to call her. I do and we get together. April Boyd is a Métis journalist for the *New Breed Journal*, and she writes an article about me for it.

From Vancouver, I go to my last destination, Terrace, British Columbia, added at the last minute because Viola Thomas, the Executive-Director of the Kermode Friendship Centre, is very persuasive about having me come to their little town in the mountains. From Montreal to Terrace, I've renewed old friendships and made new friends. I've been so lucky to have such strong articulate sisters to support me.

CHAPTER 20

THE WINNIPEG COALITION ON NATIVE CHILD Welfare has managed to get the provincial government to begin negotiations for a Native-run child and family services agency. Louise Champagne, who has been active in organizing community meetings, invites me to sit in on the discussions just to watch and take notes as I please. At last I get a close look at one of the sources of cunning trickery. With nothing to lose the government side seems to have already decided what it will give. Eventually our side splits, as a few demand a mandated agency, that is, one with the power to apprehend children. The government side says maybe later but not now. The majority on our side will accept a non-mandated agency because the need to get something started is so urgent.

From these discussions the Ma-Mawi-Wi-Chi-Itata Centre is born. I am asked to sit on the board of directors. The name, suggested by another board member, means "we all help each other." I like this idea. It's different from having all those white social workers "helping" my family and feeding us the idea that we will always need help from white people. At Ma-Mawi-Wi-Chi-Itata, if a family needs help, the Centre helps and in turn the family helps the Centre in some way, even if it's just taking part in community events. By bringing families together, the Centre is attempting to lessen people's feelings of isolation. As the first board members, we brainstorm other ways the Centre can help improve the quality of life for Winnipeg's Native families.

MEANWHILE VIRGINIA LEAVES Pemmican to have a baby and she'll be gone for about a year. I've been in contact with Marla, my former foster sister, and I hire her to fill in. She works on accounts receivable, processes book orders, and helps me with marketing, leaving me to do the balance of the work in administration, acquisitions, and production. The president of MMF, Don McIvor, offers to sell Pemmican Publications to us for a dollar, but I feel that it belongs to the Métis people, and should not be privately owned. We turn them down with much regret — after all, we can afford the price.

THE ASSOCIATION OF MANITOBA BOOK Publishers has successfully lobbied the provincial government to have Manitoba books in all schools and public libraries. We fill these orders; but a political problem develops with *In Search of April Raintree*. We had inadvertently allowed the distributor to send them to elementary school libraries and I could certainly understand the objections. After all, I had written it for an adult readership. When the Native Education Branch asks if I would edit the book for school use, I agree without hesitation.

I AM INVITED TO a Native writers' workshop on the first weekend of March. The Native Education Branch arranged it, although the idea came from Bernelda Wheeler, who had participated in similar workshops held by Maria Campbell. Bernelda had been the well-known host, producer, and journalist for *Our Native Land*, a highly successful national CBC radio program, which focused on Native people and issues. In spite of its success CBC radio ended the program in 1982.

Among the other participants are Dorine Thomas, who first accepted my novel for Pemmican; Don Floyd, who will be producing a video about me called *In Search of Beatrice Culleton*; and Bernelda Wheeler and her son, Jordan. Our stories are to be for students from kindergarten to grade 3. Resource people provide us with a list of story patterns most useful in child learning. After a second workshop Bernelda has three publishable stories. (I come up with nothing.) I arrange for Pemmican to co-publish Bernelda's books with the Native Education Branch.

The MMF hold elections in early 1984 and Yvon Dumont replaces Don McIvor as president. I am sorry to see Don leave, as he was the salt of the earth — and I just love salt. The MMF moves its offices and our new office is twice as large as our previous space.

ON A PERSONAL LEVEL, we also move, from St. Norbert to a duplex in Elmwood. We rent out the upstairs and begin renovating the lower unit for ourselves. I want a Jacuzzi bathtub so we completely redo the bathroom. After we've finished with the main floor, we tackle the basement — I've discovered that renovating is a lot more fun than writing and publishing.

AT THE BEGINNING of September I attend the Canadian Women's Music and Cultural Festival, where I first meet Alanis Obomsawin. After our session on stage, Bradley Bird of the *Winnipeg Free Press* does a short interview with me and asks to do a longer one. I invite him to come to Pemmican Publications where he interviews both Marla and me. A half-page article appears in the *Winnipeg Free Press* and a condensed version appears across the country through Associated Press.

IN OCTOBER I'M AT THE University of North Dakota for the Outsider's Conference. The three other speakers are also writers, Louise Erdrich, William P. Kinsella, and James Welch. I am honoured to be on the same program as Louise, and I'm so impressed with her when we meet. She is successful, yet completely down to earth. I wasn't familiar with James Welch, but I had heard of Kinsella and had read his *Dance Me Outside*. Kinsella is in hot water over appropriation of Native voice, an issue raised by eastern writers such as Lenore Keshig-Tobias. That's too bad because his book reminded me of my brother and I had enjoyed it. However, as a new-ish "Native writer," I feel I have to support the Native position, although I don't quite understand the subtleties of the reasoning behind it. The next morning William Kinsella and I take the same flight back to Winnipeg. He turns out to be very nice and very funny.

At Pemmican we have never asked writers if they are Native; to do so would seem like reverse racism. I had chosen to publish children's books purely for their ability to entertain and to show Native families in contemporary settings. They were also the best manuscripts available at the time. Now I will have to be on guard for appropriation of voice.

So what exactly is appropriation of Native voice? I simplify it for myself: if a non-Native is writing as if he/she were Native, that is appropriation. If non-Native people copyright Indian stories or legends that have been passed down through oral traditions, well that would go beyond appropriation. That would be blatant theft. Native people have been voiceless for so long that appropriating our voice is an outrage. It shows a lack of understanding of our history and disrespect for our needs. Our solution, besides making potential 'appropriationists' aware of what they're doing, is for more of us to write our own stories. The problem is that we need more publishers for these stories.

IN NOVEMBER I BEGIN work on the revised school edition of *In Search of April Raintree*. If there are protocols for revising books, I haven't learned of any, so I concentrate on the objective: to provide an edition more suitable for high school students. My aim is simple: to entice people — especially those who would not normally read about us — into reading books about Native peoples, then hunger for more. In December 1984, *April Raintree* is published.

LOUISE CHAMPAGNE and some of the trainees from the Métis Economic Development Training Program (MEDTP) organize Coffee Expressions, as a way for families from our community to gather on Friday evenings. Anyone is welcome to sing, play an instrument, tell stories, or read poetry. I get Debbie to read from Pemmican's children's books to the little ones, who gather around her when she does so. These evenings come to an end only because the organization that offered the space has to move.

Although some MEDTP ventures failed because of lack of funding and support, three still operate today: a grocery store called Neechi

Foods, Payuk Inter-Tribal Co-op Housing, and Niigaanaki Daycare Centre. The businesses operate as co-operatives, the most community-oriented model. The all-encompassing training program had been impressive and the students had always seemed enthusiastic about it, because they owned it. The program had not been imposed on them. Pemmican publishes *Currents of Change: Métis Economic Development*, which describes how this training program was established and administered.

Working with the Native Education Branch, Pemmican publishes a legend from northern Manitoba, told by Norway House writer, Murdo Scribe. He is recording local stories and legends in the hope that they will give today's youth a sense of pride in their ancestors. The legend tells of how, long ago before man, the animals decide to divide time and share summer and winter. We get lucky in finding Terry Gallagher who produces brilliant black-and-white illustrations. Thanks to the Native Education Branch we are also able to publish *Murdo's Story* in Cree and in Ojibwe.

In 1985, the centenary of the Métis rebellion, Terry Gallagher's illustrations win the 1985 Canada Council Award for Children's Illustrations, the MMF honors me with The Order of the Sash, and my novella, *Spirit of the White Bison*, is published.

Everything is on track at Pemmican. We're on target with the books we plan to publish and our sales have more than doubled each year. All our children's books have been on the Children's Choice list, a special recommendation from the Children's Book Centre; and many of our books have had to be reprinted. We are doing so well that our accountant has to remind me that Pemmican is a non-profit business. Virginia has returned, Marla stays on, and we pay half the salary for the trainees, whom the Core Initiatives training program sends to us from time to time.

I'm not sure I like the numerous short-term training programs such as Core as they don't seem to lead to full-time, well-paying jobs. Community workers call them bandage solutions. The concept of the MEDTP would have been better because it included a run-your-own business component; but it didn't get ongoing funding. I do recognize that for the trainees, short-term training programs, even if they may be a way to sustain cunning trickery, are better than nothing. By now I know the proper term for cunning trickery: it's systemic racism.

ON THE HOME FRONT, the news isn't good. I learn the truth about Bill's life away from home. His cousin Fred and his latest girlfriend Linda invite us for supper. While Fred and Bill watch television, Linda tells me how she met Fred at a party and they all thought Bill was also single because of the way he carried on.

Although I'm seething with anger on our way home, I decide not to talk to Bill about what I've been told. After all Linda has only confirmed what I merely turned a blind eye to. Billy is almost 18, but Debbie is only 13. To disrupt her life at this age might be traumatic. Unless Bill leaves us, I make the difficult decision to wait it out for at least another three years. After all, for 11 years, he has been a good father to our children. And if he had any decency — or maybe some self-control — he would have been good to me too.

ONE HOT JUNE AFTERNOON, John Tootoosis comes to Pemmican to get copies of his books to take to the Elders' Conference on Education, at the Convention Centre. We drop what we're doing, get books together, and Marla drives us over to the Convention Centre.

John introduces me, saying that I will speak at the conference about education. What? What can I possibly say to Elders and educators? Then I realize I need to honour the faith this man has in me and, amazingly, words come. I talk about the need to have more children's books, more books that will bring Indian people into today's world. We have to lobby for books to be published in Aboriginal languages. Government funding is now available only for English- and French-language books. Native education needs to start well before high school, college, and university. We need to instill a positive image early: no matter what a child's home life may be like, these books will make them smile and want to learn.

THE ASSOCIATION OF MANITOBA Book Publishers lobbies the Manitoba Arts Council for funding for the computers, software, and the training that are out of reach for most Manitoba publishers. Computers would save a lot of time with grant applications and budgets; they even have publishing software that would do away with the time-consuming manual labour of typesetting. In early 1987, the computer component is approved. A computer whiz programs my sales-tracking needs into the new accounting system. Now each invoice will automatically be posted to the accounts receivable journal, inventory, sales tracking, and authors' records.

WITH ALL THE CHILDREN'S books from our joint efforts having been published, the Native Education staff organizes a community celebration. The event is held at the Indian & Métis Friendship Centre. Besides guest speakers from the education department and the MMF, we invite the authors and illustrators. After the speeches and the feast, Indian dancers perform the Round Dance in their honour. It's all very moving and I'm gratified to see the Centre filled with parents and children.

IN JUNE 1987 VIRGINIA and I attend the Canadian Booksellers convention in Toronto. One evening after supper we have nothing planned, so Virginia phones a friend who lives in Toronto. There's only one person I would want to see — George Moehring, from my George Brown College days although he's probably living in Hamilton now. Nonetheless, I look in the phone book and find a listing for him. I call and tell him who I am — does he remember me? He says of course he remembers me. We meet in the coffee shop at my hotel and talk long into the night. The next night we have supper together, and the following morning Virginia and I return to Winnipeg. George and I talk on the phone almost every night.

My plan had been to leave Bill only after Debbie turns 16; but Bill has been inadvertently helping me make the break. For almost a year he's been critical, bossy, and in such a foul mood, that we can't wait for him to go back on the road. At the end of August I tell him that Debbie and I will be moving to Toronto. I don't know what, if anything, will happen between George and me. I do know that having made that initial phone call to George, I can no longer live with Bill.

BERNELDA WHEELER and I have a last meal together before I leave for Toronto. She has been working for Arrowfax and is excited about their just-completed *First Nations Tribal Directory*. It contains listings of Native governments, organizations, programs, and businesses in the United States and Canada. I buy two — one for Pemmican and one for myself. I ask her why this new term, "Aboriginal," is better than "Native." She explains that Aboriginal groups demanded the change, and it was incorporated in the 1983 amendment to the Constitution Act of 1982. In the Indian Act of 1876, if you were "native," you weren't even a "person." I make the comment that the Métis aren't really Aboriginal people. With a mischievous grin, she says that's why Indian people call themselves the First Nations.

Then we get on to fun stuff, as we both like to laugh a lot. She tells me of a recent visit to a rural town to do a reading, and two older ladies came in early, all excited to see her. She was quite pleased until she learned they were expecting her to read their tea leaves or Tarot cards.

In turn I tell her about a reading at an elementary school. Afterwards a little boy asked, "Did you write that book?" I answered yes, thinking that he was going to tell me that he liked it. Instead he asked, "Well, how come you have to read from it? Don't you remember what you wrote?"

MY LAST VISITS ARE with Mom and Dad. We end up talking about Mom's family and I'm surprised to learn that Mom didn't have two older sisters but five, and that after her mother died, her father remarried and they had three boys. I knew only one first cousin — Hilda Spence — and she was closer to Mom's age than mine. Later Mom and I play gin rummy and she wins, as usual. What is unusual is that I came to the visit believing I had few relatives and I leave knowing I have almost 70.

When I visit Dad I ask him about his family. He doesn't seem to know much, only that his father came from North Dakota. His side remains a mystery. My visits with Dad are like our family visits when I was a child. At first we don't seem to have that much in common. Then gradually I relax and we find ourselves joking and laughing. I love hearing Mom and Dad laugh.

When I was young, in spite of how I had rejected them, I felt that there was something very special about my parents. Later I dismissed that feeling, but then much later I realized I had been driven to write *In Search of April Raintree*, in part because of them. Both my parents have a childlike trust and an innocence that had been passed to me. Both believe in the best of the Roman Catholic Church and Dad still attends Sunday Mass. In spite of all they have been through, the Church is able to give them comfort. I'm grateful for that.

I CHOOSE THE LAST day of October to leave, and because I know that Debbie will want to celebrate her birthday and Halloween with her friends, she will fly to Toronto the following Tuesday.

On Saturday morning George arrives in Winnipeg. I meet him at the airport, and we head to Toronto in my car packed with everything I want to take. As I leave Winnipeg behind, I feel that I am saying good-bye to publishing and writing. I feel I have given Pemmican Publications a good foundation and that with the right people running it — Virginia is to take over as managing editor — it can become highly successful. With that, I figure I can walk away from it all.

I also tell myself I always knew I wasn't going to write another novel like *In Search of April Raintree*. I have sometimes felt guilty at being celebrated as a writer because real writers have a single-minded ambition, maybe even an obsession to write; and I don't. I'll probably still involve myself in social activism because I now know that's who I am. But I'll work quietly behind the scenes.

Unknown, Auntie Ada (seated) & Mom, 1984

Me, John Oleksiuk and Mary Scorer at University of Manitoba event, 1986

Mom & Dad, 1994

As a boy, George used to go to camp in Cuxhaven. We're on a ferry on the North Sea, 1993

Vacationing in Cuxhaven, Germany, on the North Sea, 1993

Mom and Dad at Métis Pavilion, Folklorama, 1995

St. Mary's Cathederal for Dad's funeral service, 1997

Debbie, George, me, Mom, my brother Eddie, and Billy, before heading
to Ste. Rose du Lac for Dad's burial, 1997

My favourite thing to do: horsebackriding, 1999

Debbie and Billy, 2001

Epilogue

G EORGE, DEBBIE, AND I HAVE to make a lot of adjustments, sometimes not very peacefully. Surprisingly I find myself going through
a time of mourning and sometimes I cry for no apparent reason. Is it for
Bill? Am I burnt out from my work at Pemmican? Is it guilt at having
torn Debbie's world apart? I think that's it. She misses Billy, her father,
and all her friends. To her, home will always be in Winnipeg and to
lessen the difficulty for her, I plan to let her spend Christmas, March
break, and summer holidays in Winnipeg. Billy stays with his father for
now but he and some friends plan to leave for British Columbia.

In August 1988 George and I get married without exchanging rings.
Such symbols don't mean anything to me and I still don't like diamonds
and gold. What counts is that we stay true to our commitment.

George has a cottage with a lot next to it. We discover we share an interest in woodworking, although neither of us has done much. We begin
making furniture for ourselves and then for other cottagers, and soon
we need a workshop. When he decides we should build on the empty
lot, I tell him that I want to design the cottage.

My design is not at all like my long-ago designs. In facing the lake,
the cottage will also face south, so all the windows and most of the doors
will face south. *Most* doors? Yes. The bungalow is 70' x 26' with an angled
extension for the dining room and kitchen. It has a walkout basement

to the lake, so we have three sliding glass doors and two entrance doors. My tipi is the living room in the centre, with large A-framed windows. Both the sun and the moon shine their magic into most of the cottage.

A heat-exchange system takes heat from the lake in winter for the furnace and water heater, and cools the house in the summer, greatly reducing our need for electricity. We build our own oak kitchen and, because I hate fabric curtains, I design manually operated interior wood shutters. When we finally get to mount them, it's magic. Thanks to George I have been able to fulfill a lifelong dream of designing a home and seeing it built.

IN LATE OCTOBER 1990 I'm invited by Pemmican to celebrate its tenth anniversary in Winnipeg. While there I ask Murray Sinclair to arrange for me to talk with women at the Portage Correctional Institution, as I have an idea for a book about women in prison. Murray was one of the Commissioners for The Aboriginal Justice Inquiry of Manitoba. Hearings had been televised and we had watched, day after day.

Back in 1989 a police officer committed suicide rather than testify at the hearing. His choice makes no sense to me. What I find chilling is the reaction of the Winnipeg police chief who claims the inquiry may claim more victims. Many officers follow his lead and blame the Aboriginal Justice Inquiry and the media for the suicide, ignoring their own role in the denial of justice for Aboriginal people.

Now when Virginia and I arrive, the prison officials seem wary. I suppose for our safety, one remains in the room throughout our visit. Even so, the inmates talk to me freely. I ask my questions, make my notes, and listen; but I'm distracted each time the prison official explains something. She is dressed for Halloween, in a scarecrow costume, her face painted black with big red lips. Every time she speaks I fixate on those moving oversized red lips and I find it really hard to keep a straight face. The absurdity of it has Virginia and me laughing practically all the way back to Winnipeg.

That evening during supper with Mom and Dad, I start thinking again about the monotone accounts by the inmates of why they were in jail and what it meant to them, and I suddenly begin to cry. Mom and

Dad look at me with surprise and alarm. I assure them that neither of them made me cry, and tell them about my visit with the inmates. It has just dawned on me that those women are powerful but don't know their own power. They are the ones who should write their stories; it's not for me to do it.

ALTHOUGH I HAD planned to live quietly, April Raintree draws me into all kinds of activities. Shortly after I'm back home in Toronto, June Callwood calls to ask me to be on the PEN board of directors. I say no, because I have no idea what PEN is. She explains that it works worldwide on behalf of writers forced into silence. It is just after the Oka crisis, and PEN wants an Aboriginal voice to oppose the Conservative government's cuts to Aboriginal media funding. June is very persuasive. As a board member the first thing I do is phone Aboriginal media people from my *First Nations Tribal Directory* to learn how the cuts have affected them.

In January 1991, I go to Ottawa with the president of PEN, John Ralston Saul, and a First Nations law student to meet with Liberal and NDP politicians. No one from the Secretary of State's office can meet with us, telling us it's because Mulroney has sent troops off to the Persian Gulf War. (Huh? This makes no sense to us.) In one of parliament's media rooms, I'm unexpectedly thrust forward to speak to the gathered reporters about the effects of the funding cuts.

The other directors of PEN are hardworking and devoted to worldwide writers; my devotion is only to Aboriginal people. When I feel I've done what I can, I resign.

ALANIS OBOMSAWIN calls one day and asks if I would be interested in writing a short film script about racism for the National Film Board. It is to be one of a series of four, called *Playing Fair,* for children in elementary school. I'm assigned to the seven-to-nine age group. I phone a nearby elementary school and they let me sit in on a few classes. I had the idea of making a child from this age group a culprit, but these little kids are so sweet to each other. One of the girls starts humming, and pretty soon the whole class is humming along. Then a little boy comes up to me and says, "We're all pigs." I go, "Huh?" He repeats, "We're all pigs in here." Then he shows me a book about the Chinese calendar: the kids were born in the Year of the Pig. There's not a racist or a bully in sight: I'll have to make older boys the culprits.

The NFB invites me to Montreal to watch the film shoot. Alanis has found Luis, a young boy who has never acted before, to be the main character. Bullying is so foreign to him that in rehearsal he asks why the older boys are being so mean to him. The other young actors explain to him it's only pretend.

Because I try to have animals in whatever I write, I have a dog in my script and when the trainer tells me his dog can growl on command, I write a growling scene into the script. At Alanis's suggestion my piece is called *Walker,* and the series wins a Gold Apple award, among others.

IN AUGUST 1991 I'M accepted to a one-month Summer Lab course at the Canadian Film Centre on the basis of my quickly written screenplay of *In Search of April Raintree.* This summer lab is an experiment, offering producing, directing, and screenwriting training to visible minorities, to engage them in commercial filmmaking. I am the only Aboriginal participant and the only screenwriter 'wannabe.' I'm also the only one who has never worked in commercial film. Although she's only worked on documentary films, Alanis is the only Aboriginal person they can find who has actually worked in film development, and is one of the lecturers. We get to direct and edit a ten-minute scene from our work. Kate Mathews and Pamela Matthews, playing April and Cheryl, help make the experience especially enjoyable.

At the end of the course we meet with the white students from the year-long training program. One of them tells us she never even noticed that we were visible minorities. For some reason, and despite once having thought being colour-blind was good, her comment angers me. I say that to deny our colour is to deny our histories, and I go on about how films of the past have either made clowns of us or killed us off. I've been so quiet and shy throughout the sessions that I stun my group into silence.

IN NOVEMBER TOMSON HIGHWAY asks if I would write a play for a spring production. He's working on *The Rose*, but it won't be ready in time. Tomson is even more persuasive than June, so I say yes. Then reality sets in. I've seen only a handful of plays in my life; and I'm hard of hearing, so I've always missed most of the dialogue. In school, I had hated having to study Shakespeare's plays, subconsciously considering this to be a form of forced assimilation. More to the point, I don't have a clue how to write a play so I go to a bookstore and buy *How to Write a Play*, by Raymond Hull.

The subject of the play is rape. Set in Winnipeg, it begins in 1989, with one of the main characters working for The Aboriginal Justice Inquiry of Manitoba, because I want people to be aware of this inquiry. It ends on June 22nd, 1990, the day Elijah Harper says, "No," and scuttles the Meech Lake Accord. (Aboriginal groups had been critical of The Accord and Mulroney had promised to deal with their concerns "later," after the Accord was signed. You know, like with the treaties.) Unlike April Raintree, the women in the play will learn martial arts, and fight back. My play is called, *Night of the Trickster.*

Art Solomon, a well-known Elder, sees it and tells one of the actresses I did a very good thing, an important thing. Coming from him that's an honour!

IN 1993 HARTMUT LUTZ, a professor at the University of Osnobruk, gets a German publisher interested in publishing a German edition of *In Search of April Raintree*. That July my German-born mother-in-law will be celebrating her 80th birthday and wants us to come to Germany with her. Hartmut arranges for me to speak at four universities in late June. The last, the university in Greifswald on the Baltic Sea, is the most interesting because of the recent reunification of Germany.

I'M IN WINNIPEG to visit my parents in the summer of 1994 and Mom makes herself tea and a snack. While I sit at the table near the window watching the neighbourhood children play street hockey, I'm reminded of how April Raintree had viewed Native kids as dirty.

At an Aboriginal conference back in Toronto a few people had recently told me of different experiences they'd had as foster children. Their stories made a buried childhood memory of my own, resurface.

When I was about five, Mrs. Chevalier told me to go wash myself. I did and when I came back she said I was still dirty. So she took some kind of liquid cleanser (not bleach) and wiped my face with it. My face began to burn and I screamed from the pain. I noticed a look of panic on her face and that scared me even more. Mr. Chevalier came to see what was wrong and she told him she was trying to clean me. He got impatient with her and said, "That's just the colour of her skin. You can't make her white." She was able to wash away the burning sensation with water.

None of this was done with the intent to hurt but it revealed how they saw me. Because of my age and the trust I had in them, I internalized the incident and never thought about it, not even in the writing of the second draft of *In Search of April Raintree*. Reflecting now, I believe this experience existed subconsciously and came through when I wrote about April as a five-year old child. I had been one of those "dirty little brown-skinned" children she despised.

Just as Mom joins me at the table, I see a cat walk through the play area and the children stop playing to allow the cat to go through. A surge of affection for these unknown children runs through me.

IN OCTOBER 1994 I get a contract as a consultant to the Royal Commission on Aboriginal Peoples (RCAP). I attend the commissioners' board meetings in Ottawa and I'm given reams of papers on Health, Education, and Social policies to read and make notes. RCAP sets me up with a computer link so I can do much of my work at home. I have access to all the hearings and round tables from across Canada held so far. The testimonies given are far more interesting than what the reports will become, because they are the voices direct from the people. One of the most striking pieces that I read is George Erasmus's reaction after asking a group of inmates how many of them were former foster wards. The proportion must have been so high that all he can say is, "My God!"

When I'm finished with my work, I read about the other issues that affect Aboriginal peoples across the country. For me they are all inter-connected. I think about Eddie and his friends being jailed numerous times for drinking under age. Yet I had never heard of police raids on non-Native groups. Jail further limits an already limited possibility of a job. Back then we had laughed about it, but now, I know the raids and the ongoing treatment of Aboriginal people are part of systemic racism.

ONE WEEKEND AT the cottage a children's story comes to me and it's about the mistreatment and the disappearance of animals. *Christopher's Folly* is published by Pemmican in 1996, under my maiden name, Beatrice Mosionier. Tanya, who's now the managing editor of Pemmican, asks me to accompany her to the Chicago convention of the American Book-sellers Association and then to the Canadian Booksellers convention in Vancouver, where I'm able to visit my son.

DAD HAS A GOOD FRIEND, Margaret Gauthier, who also lives in his building and besides watching television together they go to bingo and events at the Friendship Centre. One day in a hurt, puzzled tone, Dad tells me that Margaret has moved out without telling him. I find out that she has died and I have to tell him.

Shortly after he is admitted to the St. Boniface Hospital with a mini-stroke. The doctor tells me that Dad's mind is going and he will never be able to live on his own again. In August when I'm in Winnipeg, Mom and I take him from the hospital to the Métis Pavilion at Folklorama. Both are delighted with the fiddling, jigs, and square dances, and they enjoy each other's company.

From the hospital, he is moved to Central Park Lodge downtown. While he can still walk, the nurses have to hide his coat and cap to keep him from heading outdoors on his own. When he can't walk anymore, Debbie or I take him in his wheelchair to the park across the street. On later visits he seems to babble and no one can understand him.

Then I take Mom on my visits. She tells me he is speaking mostly in a combination of Saulteaux and French, which she understands quite well. We play cards, and Dad makes some jokes in English that have Mom and me laughing. Mom's presence has a very good effect on him.

On February 24th, 1997, I receive an early morning phone call from a nurse at the Misericordia Hospital. My father had been brought in during the night with a thrombosis that has caused a pulmonary embolism. He has passed away. He was 87 years old and in poor health, and I had tried to prepare for the eventuality of his death. I think with death being so final, one can never really prepare for it. The funeral is held at St. Mary's Cathedral, the church he had attended when he was living on his own.

Dad's wish is to be buried in Ste. Rose du Lac so I make plans to return in May to bury his ashes. I also know that another wish of his would have been to see his son one more time, but I'd always felt that was Eddie's choice. Now I'm hoping that Eddie will be able to come to Ste. Rose du Lac with us. However, I last talked to him in 1983 and have no idea how to find him.

Back in Toronto, determined that I *will* find him, I dig up my old *First Nations Tribal Directory* and on Thursday night I fax a note to First Nations band offices in British Columbia: if anyone knows of Eddie Mosionier's whereabouts, please tell him to get in touch with his sister. I give our home and cottage phone numbers, and plan to continue with my faxing the following Monday. A few days later I'm talking to Eddie. Wow!

In May we all go to Ste. Rose du Lac to bury my father's ashes. Eddie had told me a long time ago that he wanted nothing to do with Mom and he's never told me why. In Ste. Rose, he seems distant with her. I will see him one more time in Vancouver in the spring of 2001. My letters to him will be returned and we will lose contact.

Only now, in writing this memoir, do I realize the positive impact that Eddie had on me. Just as Cheryl was April's teacher and guide, so Eddie was mine. When I was writing my first novel, his spirit must have been right there with me.

IN 1999 PORTAGE & Main Press, having purchased the rights to my first three Pemmican books, publishes *In Search of April Raintree, the Critical Edition*. Nine essays by academics are added to the novel. (I want Professor Hartmut Lutz to be a contributor, but the editor is unable to track him down.) Their essays are sent to me for comments and approval and because I decide that the contributors are entitled to have their say, whether I agree with them or not, I approve them all.

THE CANADA COUNCIL calls and urges me to apply for a grant. Okay. I do have a novel in mind, inspired by the moonlight outside our cottage and visions of wolves running through the woods before all the cottages were built. I decide to tackle the first child molestation in my life. Since I want to set the novel in the foothills of the Rockies, I visit Fort St. John, B.C. with Debbie. *In the Shadow of Evil* will be published in December 2000 by Theytus Books, an Aboriginal publishing house in Penticton, B.C., under Beatrice Culleton Mosionier.

AS A CHILD, I KNEW I would do something special. I never thought I would become a writer. In rejecting my parents I rejected my heritage and buried the instincts of my childhood, but they would always be part of me. Today I am still the same person I was when I was three and realized I was alive. I like myself. I might not like some of the things I've done, or didn't do, but I've always liked myself.

IN THE FALL OF 1999, I visit Mom in Winnipeg. Her hip is bothering her, so I take her out for a walk in Dad's wheelchair. She tells me the nurse who comes to take care of her wants her to go live at Central Park Lodge. She likes living independently. I call her nurse and she's concerned that my mother's cataracts are returning, her hip problem is getting worse, and she's on several medications. My mother, she says, should be moved to a care home. I can't decide what to do. Just because I would never want to go to such a place doesn't mean I should impose my wishes on Mom.

Just before I leave to return to Toronto, she tells me about a recent dream. In this dream she was in bed sleeping when she felt a hard poke on her leg, which woke her up. She was startled to see a man all dressed in black standing over her. She was so scared that she woke up from the dream. The dream seemed so real, that Mom got up to check the door and found it was still locked. As she's telling me this, chills run up and down my back.

DURING THE NIGHT on December 18th, 1999, Mom's heart gives out. I feel she has let herself die. In her early years she had been institutionalized in residential schools, and I feel she was determined she would not be institutionalized again for the remainder of her days.

I could have learned so much from Mom and Dad, but I thought they had nothing to offer. Then in 2001, I find out that I can get the tapes from the National Film Board put on cassette. That's when I finally get to hear Mom's story, thanks to the interview with Alanis Obomsawin that begins each part of this memoir.

To a certain point, my life had been parallel to her life, almost as if we walked hand in hand. Then I let go of her hand to go my own way. Part of my salvation was my decision to stay away from alcohol, especially in my vulnerable times. Another part was writing the elements of April's life — and to a smaller extent, Cheryl's — that parallel my own.

In a scene from the novel, an Elder puts her hand on April's. As I wrote that scene I recalled having felt such a touch, one that was spiritual and full of warmth, compassion, and love. I know now it was my mother's hand.